God's Presence in the
Eucharist and in the World

D1602532

Also by Cardinal Müller
from Sophia Institute Press:

Benedict and Francis
Vatican Confidential
Roman Encounters

Gerhard Cardinal Müller

GOD'S PRESENCE
in the EUCHARIST
and in the WORLD

Meditations for Union with God

Translated from the German
by Susan Johnson

SOPHIA INSTITUTE PRESS
Manchester, New Hampshire

Sophia Institute Press
Box 5284, Manchester, NH 03108
1-800-888-9344
www.SophiaInstitute.com

Sophia Institute Press® is a registered trademark of Sophia Institute.

paperback ISBN 979-8-88911-248-8
ebook ISBN 979-8-88911-249-5

Library of Congress Control Number: 2024937208

First printing

Contents

God's Presence in the Eucharist and in the World

Translator's note on "noninclusive" language: The word *man* with masculine pronouns is used throughout for *Mensch* but is to be understood inclusively as male and female individuals or humanity as a whole. Where this is done, it is solely for clarity and in order to avoid clumsy formulations or plurals where the individual is meant. It also accords with the usage in many of the quoted texts.

Introduction

The purpose of spiritual exercises

In 2021, I was invited to Our Lady of Clear Creek Abbey in Oklahoma to preach the annual retreat for its sixty monks. The theme running through the retreat was the Real Presence of God in creation, in the Church, and in the Eucharist. In the autumn of that year, I led the same Spiritual Exercises with four hundred priests in the Polish diocese of Tarnów. But why do we speak of preaching a retreat rather than just giving one, just as, in Christian art, we say that icons are written and not—as one might expect—painted?

The answer is simple. A retreat is not about offering an intellectual exposition of theological facts, but it aims rather to lead us to a Person in whom we place all our hope in life and in death. A retreat is an interplay between preacher and hearer in proclaiming and bearing witness to the mystery of our redemption through Jesus Christ and our being elevated to the status of children and friends of God. In this way, it resembles the beginning of Jesus' public ministry. One disciple led another to Jesus with the words "Come and see" (John 1:46). But the sole goal of our encounter with Jesus of Nazareth can be the understanding that "Rabbi, you are the Son of God! You are the King of Israel!" (John 1:49). And Jesus, the Word made flesh, the Son of the Father, allows us to live with Him so that we may grow familiar with Him. We are comforted in the trials and tribulations of this world-time with the prospect of salvation: "In my Father's house there are many dwelling-places.... Those who love me will keep my word, and my Father will love them, and we will come to them and make our home with them" (John 14:2, 23).

It is this truth that we have to make our own, both spiritually and in the reality of our lives as disciple of the crucified and risen Lord. The figure of Jesus should be imprinted on our souls and expressed in our lives.

Everyone who preaches a retreat would wish to address the following heartfelt request to those who are listening to his words, which can be no more than the medium of the direct Word of God to every believer: "Let the same mind be in you that was in Christ Jesus" (Phil. 2:5).

We have St. Ignatius of Loyola to thank for elaborating the method of the "Spiritual Exercises to conquer oneself and regulate one's life without determining oneself through any tendency that is disordered." At the beginning of his book of Spiritual Exercises, he offers us the following definition:

> By this name of Spiritual Exercises is meant every way of examining one's conscience, of meditating (*meditar*), of contemplating (*contemplar*), of praying vocally and mentally, and of performing other spiritual actions.... For as strolling, walking and running are bodily exercises, so every way of preparing and disposing (*disponer*) the soul to rid itself of all the disordered tendencies (*affectiones*), and, after it is rid, to seek and find the Divine Will as to the management (*disposición*) of one's life for the salvation of the soul, is called a Spiritual Exercise.... For it is not knowing much,

but realising (*sentir*) and relishing (*gustar*) things interiorly (*internamente*), that contents and satisfies the soul.[1]

Here Ignatius is unmistakably drawing on the Pauline image of the race (1 Cor. 9:24-27; Heb. 12:1-3) or spiritual battle (the militia of Christ) (Eph. 6:10-17). However, the goal of these exertions and sacrifices is not to triumph over "enemies of blood and flesh" (Eph. 6:12) as in a "war,"[2] but rather to conquer oneself and one's egoism, to vanquish the feeling of being lost in the world and the distress of having forgotten God (*Gottvergessenheit*).

The sole and entire purpose of Spiritual Exercises can be expressed in the words of St Paul:

I want to know Christ and the power of his resurrection and the sharing of his sufferings by becoming like him in his death, if somehow I may attain the resurrection from the dead.

[1] Ignatius of Loyola, *The Spiritual Exercises*, trans. Elder Mullan, S.J. (New York: P.J. Kenedy and Sons, 1914); cf. Hugo Rahner, *Ignatius von Loyola als Mensch und Theologe* (Freiburg i. Br.: Basel, Vienna, 1964) (English: *Ignatius the Theologian* [New York: Herder and Herder,1968]); Erich Przywara, *Deus semper maior. Theologie der Exerzitien*, 3 vols., Freiburg i. Br.: Herder, 1938-1940; Karl Rahner, *Ignatianischer Geist. Schriften zu den Exerzitien und zur Spiritualität des Ordensgründers*: SW 13, Freiburg i. Br.: Herder, 2006.

[2] The military theorist General Carl von Clausewitz, in *Vom Kriege* (1832), Hamburg 2021, offers the following definition: "War therefore is an act of violence intended to compel our opponent to fulfil our will." That is the escalating interaction of evil, which continually breeds only evil. But of Jesus it is said that His desire was to "create in himself one new humanity in place of the two, thus making peace, and [to] reconcile both groups to God in one body through the cross, thus putting to death that hostility through it" (Eph. 2:15-16).

God's Presence in the Eucharist and in the World

> Not that I have already obtained this or have already reached the goal; but I press on to make it my own, because Christ Jesus has made me his own.... but this one thing I do: forgetting what lies behind and straining forward to what lies ahead, I press on towards the goal for the prize of the heavenly call of God in Christ Jesus. (Phil. 3:10–14)

Spiritual exercises are remedies against the feeling of nihilistic lostness in the boundless expanse of space and time. We are warned against the deceptive sense of a nirvana-like merging with the absolute All-One, as in Baruch de Spinoza's (1632–1677) divine *Allnatur*, i.e., the unique substance of the universe (*Deus sive substantia sive natura*). Christian mysticism and ascesis are the opposite of self-referential narcissism and pious self-indulgence on an ego trip. They are not wellness programs for the soul that is "swinging" in the hammock of subjectivism. There is just one thing we can learn from Eastern mysticism's suprapersonal—in reality, apersonal—transcendence into nothingness, and that is how to totally overcome it in favour of a personal encounter with the God of triune love.

The great Plotinus's (AD 205–270) Neoplatonic mysticism of the suprapersonal One beyond Being was understood by the Church Fathers as representing what was sensed and longed for by philosophers, who loved wisdom and were capable of striving after it simply because they were beginning to be suffused by it. In this way, they overcame the pagan resentment of the idea of God's presence in our flesh by turning it into a mysticism of personal love between Thou and Thou. Mediated through His assumed human nature, we are taken into (sacramentally and personally) the relation of the eternal Son to the Father in the community of the Holy Spirit. Christian spirituality originates in the eternal being and nature of God. It takes its immeasurable measure from the love that is God in the unity of Father, Son, and Holy Spirit. We would not seek God if He had not already found us in order that we might find ourselves in Him. On the Areopagus at Athens—which represents the whole of the Greek mind's search for truth, from the myth of the Orphics to the logos of the Pre-Socratics, to Socrates, Plato, and Aristotle—Paul put into words the marriage of reason and revelation, of nature and grace: "that they would search for God, and perhaps grope for him and find him—though indeed he is not far from each one of us, for 'In him we live and move and have our being'; as even some of your poets have said, 'For we are indeed his offspring'"—his génos (Acts 17:27–28).

We are no longer "slaves to the elemental powers"—as the neo-pagan "religions" would like to force us once again to be. Rather, we are ransomed from the nihilistic law of impermanence because we have become children of God. Paul says to us Christians: "And because you are children, God has sent the Spirit of his Son into our hearts, crying, 'Abba! Father!' So you are no longer a slave but a child, and if a child then also an heir, through God" (Gal. 4:6–7).

It is not the overly pious stirring of the emotions but rather the freeing of the mind and the will from the golden cage of self-reference that is the goal and thus also the path to the fresh air of the objective, the real, the existing (*Seiend*), the concrete and the corporeal. In the Triune God, *theologia cognitiva* and *theologia affectiva* are primordially (*ur-sprünglich*) united in the community of the Word and the Spirit.

With Jesus, we lift our eyes to Heaven and hear His voice saying: "Father, the hour has come; glorify your Son so that the Son may glorify you, since you have given him authority over all people, to give eternal life to all whom you have given him. And this is eternal life, that they may know you, the only true God, and Jesus Christ whom you have sent" [John 17:1–3]). It is about knowing God in his *Word* and about His love-giving *Spirit*. He awaits our response of love for *Him* in the Spirit of the Father and the Son.

"Do not be conformed to this world, but be transformed by the renewing of your minds, so that you may discern what is the will of God—what is good and acceptable and perfect" (Rom. 12:2).

We are prepared for the inner and outer man to be molded into conformity with Christ in the Holy Spirit. "Therefore be imitators of God, as beloved children, and live in love, as Christ loved us and gave himself up for us, a fragrant offering and sacrifice to God" (Eph. 5:1-2).

Let us see the whole existence and life of the earthly Jesus as the human mediation of immediacy to God. For He tells us: "Whoever has seen me has seen the Father" (John 14:9).

St. Ignatius placed the prayer Anima Christi at the beginning of his Spiritual Exercises. With it we open our hearts to "the Son of God, who loved me and gave himself for me" (Gal. 2:20)—"a fragrant offering and sacrifice to God" (Eph. 5:2).

> Soul of Christ, sanctify me.
> Body of Christ, save me.
> Blood of Christ, inebriate me.
> Water from the side of Christ, wash me.
> Passion of Christ, strengthen me.
> O Good Jesus, hear me.
> Within Your wounds hide me.
> Permit me not to be separated from You.
> From the wicked foe, defend me.
> At the hour of my death, call me
> and bid me come to You,
> That with Your saints I may praise You
> For ever and ever. Amen.

Prologue

His name is Immanuel:
God with us

Matthew 1:23

Against the idea of God's remoteness from the world or His closeness in worldless inwardness, it should be noted that, in the Christian sense, God's transcendence does not mean He lacks any relationship to the world, as is the case with Aristotle's first, unmoved mover. Knowing God's transcendence means experiencing the freedom of the God who is totally independent of the world and wishes to enter into a personal relationship of love with us. He alone can ask with commanding confidence: "Am I a God near by, says the LORD, and not a God far off?" (Jer. 23:23).

God, the totally Other — *totaliter aliud* — is the same one who bears the name:

Immanuel — God with us.

The wholly Other is also the non-other, the *non-aliud*. He is one of us.

Christ Jesus, "though he was in the form of God, did not regard equality with God as something to be exploited, but emptied himself, taking the form of a slave, being born in human likeness … being found in human form" (Phil. 2:6-7). This is the mystery of God's Incarnation, which is revealed in the divine-human unity of Christ, the Son of God, the Second Person of the Trinity. The faith of the Church formulates this theandric mystery in the dogma of the hypostatic union of the two natures of the true divinity and true humanity of Christ.

The Son of the Virgin Mary, conceived of the Holy Spirit, is the Son of the eternal Father made man. In His human nature (with an individual soul and body) we experience and recognize the nearness of the triune God. Jesus the Christ is the God-with-us, the *Deus nobiscum* (cf. Matt. 1:23).

When the risen Lord sends out His disciples to preach the gospel and to communicate grace symbolically in Baptism and the other sacraments, He reveals Himself as the *Christus praesens*, the head of the Church and of the whole cosmos: "And remember, I am with you always, to the end of the age—*et ecce ego vobiscum sum omnibus diebus, usque ad consummationem saeculi*" (Matt. 28:20).

According to the Catholic Faith, the sacraments are signs that bring about what they signify. And so the corporeal, sensorially mediated Real Presence in the Church, the Body of Christ, is instrumentally necessary for salvation. "As the assumed nature inseparably united to him, serves the Divine Word as a living organ of salvation, so, in a similar way, does the visible social structure of the Church serve the Spirit of Christ, who vivifies it, in the building up of the body."[3] For the Church is the Body of Christ both in her social form, as a community of faith, hope, and love, and her hierarchical-sacramental constitution. In a sermon to mark the feast of the Ascension, Pope Leo the Great provided the answer to the question of how the incarnate Son of God, who, after His Resurrection from the dead, is seated at the right hand of the Father in Heaven, is visibly present: "And so that which till

---

[3] Second Vatican Council, Dogmatic Constitution on the Church *Lumen gentium* (November 21, 1964), no. 8.

then was visible of our Redeemer was changed into a sacramental presence, and that faith might be more excellent and stronger, sight gave way to doctrine, the authority of which was to be accepted by believing hearts enlightened with rays from above."[4]

It is possible only under exceptional circumstances for an individual Christian believer to partake of the inner reality of the grace of the sacraments in a purely spiritual way through the divine virtues of faith, hope, and love; such a case would be if the person in question had a legitimate and grave reason for being unable to be physically present at the ecclesial assembly and its Divine Liturgy. But grace in its sacramental form is mediated only when the candidate for Baptism, Confirmation, or the Sacrament of Holy Orders is personally physically present and when the minister of the respective sacrament physically touches the candidate with the matter of the particular sacrament: water, oil of anointing, laying on of hands. "Truly our fellowship is with the Father and with his Son Jesus Christ" (1 John 1:3) only through the apostles and their successors proclaiming and witnessing to us what they *saw* with their eyes, *heard* with their ears, and *touched* with their hands: "the word of life ... the eternal life that was with the Father and was revealed to us" (1 John 1:1–2).

Only a Platonic-dualistic or Gnostic-Manichaean pre-understanding or one based altogether on a spirit-nature dialectic can devalue the Incarnation into nothing more than a mere metaphor for the presence of God in our subjective world of ideas. In such a case, the sacraments are then regarded as simply secondary supports of a transcendental union with God in the consciousness or intuition of religious feelings and not as what they really are: namely, physically touching God and real communion with God in our flesh.

[4]   Leo the Great, *Sermo* 74, 2.

God's Presence in the Eucharist and in the World

The way the mediation of grace works is also different in services in which participants are physically present and in virtual liturgies. Whereas physical participation in the Sacrifice of the Mass obtains sanctifying grace ex opere operato (i.e., objectively), intentional participation in the Mass via television can communicate helping grace only ex opere operantis (i.e., in subjective piety). Liturgy participated in physically mediates sanctifying grace sacramentally, whereas with virtual participation, we are given helping grace only by virtue of our pious disposition. For we do not partake sacramentally of Christ's sacrifice on the Cross and cannot receive Holy Communion in our mouths.

Nevertheless, a truth of faith that must not be overlooked states that it is possible for the *res sacramenti* [reality of the sacrament] to be granted to believers if, for example, they are unable, through no fault of their own, to receive sacramental Baptism and absolution but intend to catch up on the sacramental mediation of salvation at the earliest opportunity. This is, however, limited to those sacraments necessary for personal salvation and does not extend to Confirmation or the celebration of the Eucharist, let alone to priestly ordination.

The essence of being a Christian does not lie in a theoretical grasp of reality and its representation in our thoughts, in an ethical life project or in a socio-ethical agenda for improving the world. What makes someone a Christian is instead his being elevated to real participation in the divine nature, which is realized in the relations of Father and Son and Holy Spirit. Through the infused divine virtues of faith, hope, and love, we cognize in the Logos God as he cognizes Himself. With the Holy Spirit in our hearts, we love God as, in the unity of Father and Son in the Holy Spirit, He is Himself love and communicates Himself to us. Thus, in faith we are dealing with the reality of God in that we are actually and really determined by the three essential mysteries of salvation: the *mysterium Trinitatis*, the *mysterium Incarnationis Verbi Divini*, and the *mysterium inhabitationis Dei in cordibus nostris.*[5]

Here we are touching on the most fundamental ontological and epistemological principles of the Catholic Faith: the reality of God in Himself and His presence with us. With reference to their most concentrated form and synthesis, we speak of the Real Presence of Christ in the Eucharist, when the God-Man is present in the Church, His social Body, under the species of bread and wine with the whole substance of His human nature and dwells among us in the Divine Person of the Logos—which is inseparable from His divine nature. The whole reality of salvation and redemption is expressed in His words of self-revelation: "I am the living bread that came down from heaven. Whoever eats of this bread will live for ever; and the bread that I will give for the life of the world is my flesh" (John 6:51).

The Council of Trent expresses the Catholic principle extremely boldly when, in the first canon of the Decree on the Sacrament of the Eucharist, it depicts the historical presence of God in the historical man Jesus of Nazareth and His actual presence in the ecclesial Body, the Church, as culminating in the sacramental Real Presence of the whole Christ in His divinity and His humanity. Only someone who confesses that in the sacrament of the Most Holy Eucharist the God-Man is "truly, really and substantially contained—*vere, realiter et substantialiter*"[6] can be accounted Catholic. Anyone who claims that Christ is contained in the Eucharist only "as in a sign or figure or by his power"—i.e., virtually—in the

---

[5] The mystery of the Trinity, the mystery of the Incarnation of the Divine Word, and the mystery of God's living in our hearts.

[6] DH 1651.

elements of bread and wine, thus denying the change of the whole substance (transubstantiation) of bread and wine into the substance of the flesh and blood of Christ, is anathematized.

God does not distance Himself from us. He does not avoid contact with us. He touches us and embraces us. "Let him kiss me with the kisses of his mouth!" (Song of Sol. 1:2). And the Son of God lifted up on the Cross draws all to Himself (see John 12:32) and opens His divine heart to them (see John 19:34). "God's love has been poured into our hearts through the Holy Spirit that has been given to us" (Rom. 5:5). To the doubting apostle Thomas, the risen Lord says: "Reach out your hand and put it in my side. Do not doubt but believe" (John 20:27). Let us then, overwhelmed by such loving care, reply with him: "My Lord and my God!" (John 20:28). Yes, we are permitted to touch God in the human body that His Son assumed from the Virgin Mary. "For it is the God who said, 'Let light shine out of darkness', who has shone in our hearts to give the light of the knowledge of the glory of God in the [human] face of Jesus Christ" (2 Cor. 4:6). The fact that the bodily presence of God in Christ, the *Verbum Incarnatum*, is the medium and goal of God's saving action and thus the essence of the Christian faith, was already pointed out by Tertullian in his work *On the Resurrection of the Dead* in the well-known words:

> *Caro cardo salutis*—the flesh is the very condition on which salvation hinges.[7]

---

[7] Tertullian, *De resurrectione mortuorum* 8, 2.

Chapter 1

In the beginning
was the Word

John 1:1

In a towering work of world literature, Johann Wolfgang von Goethe (1749-1832), the greatest German poet, has the hero of his tragedy struggle to translate the most fundamental proposition of Sacred Scripture and mankind's entire intellectual history: Ἐν ἀρχῇ ἦν ὁ λόγος — *in principio erat verbum.* "In the beginning was the Word, and the Word was with God, and the Word was God" (John 1:1). Therein lies the whole truth of the Christian faith and "the beginning of the good news of Jesus Christ, the Son of God" (Mark 1:1).

The magister "Faust" is a mediocre professor who does not shy away from magic, esotericism, and gnosis or New Age, a brooder who wants to "understand whatever / Binds the world's innermost core together."[8] The school that he supposes will teach him the most profound insights into being is not real life of the kind millions of people have to cope with, fluctuating between a daily life filled with toil and suffering and high times full of hope and love. In his cramped, dusty study, this loner works his way upward

---

[8] Johann Wolfgang von Goethe, *Faust* I, Szene: Nacht. In einem hochgewölbten, engen gotischen Zimmer. English trans. A. S. Kline (2003), Poetry in Translation, https://www.poetryintranslation. com/klineasfaust.php.

from dry book knowledge into the airless space of ideology. In the twilight zone between science and magic, he loses touch with the ground of reality beneath his feet. His soul soars up in a flight of fancies and feelings from the lowlands of everyday life into the lofty sphere of concepts of the True, the Good, and the Beautiful. In the sentimental euphoria experienced at this high altitude, a sense of the supernatural suddenly opens up to him. His longing to understand Being drives him to open the fundamental text of revelation. He wants to render the New Testament from the original Greek "into my beloved German." What he means here is not "German" in the philological sense of a specific European language but rather as the educated world of subjective, objective, and absolute idealism in German philosophy, in Romanticism and classicism in literature and humanist culture. The Christian message had been left behind as a supposedly outgrown stage in the evolution of human consciousness. Enlightened, taking pride in reason and believing in progress, humanity had stepped out of the dark Middle Ages into the bright new age of enlightened thinking. At last, the moral heights had been scaled where the autonomous human being is his own creator and God. People no longer lived in gratitude and with thanksgiving from the fullness of grace through which God makes us perfect. In order to circumvent the necessity of grace for man's perfection, we modestly limit ourselves—so ran the new creed—to the infinite quest for the divine. But the divine beyond the personal God of the Judeo-Christian tradition is forbidden to assault us with a concrete claim to truth and come so close to us that we have to decide whether to submit our intellect and will to Him completely in childlike trust and obedience.[9] On

[9] See Second Vatican Council, Dogmatic Constitution on Divine Revelation *Dei verbum* (November 18, 1965), no. 5.

the way to humanity's self-perfection, belief in the God of Jesus Christ is replaced with belief in boundless moral and technological progress. One needs only to recall the law of three stages developed by the French critic of religion and self-appointed high priest of the new religion of positivism Auguste Comte (1798–1857), the law that sees humanity as developing analogously to the human maturation process from an immature child to an autonomous adult. This development takes place in three stages: from the theological-fictive stage via the metaphysical-abstract phase to the final positive-scientific state. Then humanity will be its own god. Then we would have left the God of metaphysics and revelation behind us as a pedagogical aid. The undertone of mockery or pity that enlightened intellectuals feel justified in using with reference to Christians can surely not escape anyone's notice here?

It is an educated bourgeois world with its malicious skepticism that has left behind it the Christian faith's claims to truth and now interprets the world pancosmically or the divine pantheistically. Or God and the world are identified with each other as the infinite horizon that can be understood only in poetic metaphors and symbolic representations.

Dr. Faust, who represents the post-Christian culture, alludes to the eternal problem of whether the original meaning is made objectively accessible in a translation or subjectively configured as a person's own respective truth. He does not consider the higher possibility of an inner relationship between ontological and logical truth, i.e., that the being (*Sein*) of truth is grounded in its own clearedness (*Gelichtetheit*) and is therefore also communicable.

Truth, on the other hand, is not an unreachable empty horizon but rather God as Person communicating with another person. Truth is not a horizon within which the light of finite minds could never dispel the darkness over the abyss of nothingness or prevent "the tragedy of humanism without God."[10] For, according to Nietzsche's statement "God is dead! God remains dead. We have killed him!,"[11] all that remains is nihilism "in its most terrible form: existence as it is, without meaning and purpose, but inevitably recurring without a finale into nothingness: 'the eternal return [*Wiederkehr*].' This is the most extreme form of nihilism: nothingness (the 'meaningless') forever!"[12]

After the excesses of the "*superman/ overman/ Übermensch*"[13] since his birth in the laboratory of self-idolatry, we should try something more modest and clothe ourselves "with the *new self* [*novum hominem*—Vulgate], created according to the likeness of God in true righteousness and holiness" (Eph. 4:24; cf. Col. 3:10).

Truth is not a product but rather the gift of enlightenment. "Now the Lord is the Spirit, and where the Spirit of the Lord is, there is freedom. And all of us, with unveiled faces, seeing the glory of the Lord as though reflected in a mirror, are being transformed

---

[10] Henri de Lubac, *Le Drame de l'Humanisme athée* [1943] (Paris, 1985); English: *The Drama of Atheist Humanism* (San Francisco: Ignatius Press, 1995) (translation of the 1983 edition, including chapters omitted from the 1949 translation).

[11] Friedrich Nietzsche, *Die fröhliche Wissenschaft* 125: *Kritische Studienausgabe* 3, ed. Giorgio Colli and M. Montinari (Munich, 1980), 481. English: *The Gay Science* (Cambridge, UK: Cambridge University Press, 2001), 120.

[12] Friedrich Nietzsche, *Nachgelassene Fragmente*, 10. Juni 1887 Nr. 6: *Kritische Studienausgabe* 12, ed. G. Colli / Mazzino Montinari, Munich 1980, 213. English: *Nietzsche's Last Twenty-Two Notebooks*: trans. Daniel Fidel Ferrer (n.p.: Kuhn von Verden Verlag, 2021), 73-74. https://ia601800.us.archive.org/35/items/fn-notebooks-1886-1889/FN%20Notebooks%201886-1889.pdf.

[13] Friedrich Nietzsche, *Also sprach Zarathustra*, Vorrede 3: *Kritische Studienausgabe* 4 (Munich, 1980), 14-15.

into the same image from one degree of glory to another; for this comes from the Lord, the Spirit" (2 Cor. 3:17-18).

Specifically, truth works as the light of God in the person of the Word, who came into the world. Christ is "true God from true God and true light from true light." Hence the Apostle could say: "For once you were darkness, but now in the Lord you are light. Live as children of light—for the fruit of the light is found in all that is good and right and true.... Everything exposed by the light becomes visible, for everything that becomes visible is light. Therefore it says, 'Sleeper, awake! Rise from the dead, and Christ will shine on you'" (Eph. 5:8-9, 13-14).

God is Himself the truth, in which He knows Himself infinitely and in which He can also communicate Himself to a finite mind. Thus, His truth can also be expressed in human language and—as a logical consequence—presented via both a print and a digital medium. The *analogia entis* [analogy of being] as the basis of the *analogia fidei* [analogy of faith] is therefore not a philosophically disguised anthropomorphism because the Creator of language is Himself the Word. God speaks to us in our language, which, as a self-expression of our being spiritual selves constitutes our being human. It is only secondarily that transcendental linguisticality becomes categorial in the actually spoken individual languages. God "sees" us with His "eyes" because He recognises Himself in the Word. He "hears" us calling and "feels" joy and suffering with us in His divine "heart" because as sympathy He is the love of the Father for the Son intrinsic in the Holy Spirit. Because our created body with its senses is an expression of our spirit or intellect (*Geist*), we are, being made hearing and seeing through the mediation of the sensorially perceived world, completely open to God's self-communication in His *Word* and *Spirit*. To the proponents of the projection theory the psalmist already issued the call:

"Understand, O dullest of the people; fools, when will you be wise? He who planted the ear, does he not hear? He who formed the eye, does he not see?" (Ps. 94:8–9).

God is Spirit and Word. Therefore, the recognition of the spiritual creature able to communicate in the Word is not a primitive transferring of human characteristics to God. Speaking analogously of God represents the insight that all sensory knowledge is rooted in man's spiritual nature, which is itself a reflection of God's being and His knowledge of Himself. "God is spirit," and therefore he can be known and worshipped "in spirit and in truth" (see John 4:23). God dwells in inaccessible light (see 1 Tim. 6:16) and no one has ever seen and known God with their natural sensory-spiritual powers of cognition. But the Son, at the Father's heart, the Word who is God, has brought us knowledge of God in Jesus Christ and thus true knowledge of God in His divine light (see John 1:8). Through the spiritual-corporeal image of Jesus' humanity, we attain to the knowledge of His divinity and thus to his relation to the Father. In the great exultation, Jesus cries, "No one knows the Son except the Father, and no one knows the Father except the Son and anyone to whom the Son chooses to reveal him" (Matt. 11:27; cf. Luke 10:22).

The universal principle of philosophical and theological knowledge per visibilia ad spiritualia applies to the incarnationally grounded act of faith and the supernatural, i.e., Spirit-infused knowledge of God's mysteries, as well as to the sacramental mediation of grace to man in his sensorial, social, and spiritual nature. Through words and signs, the human spirit—in accordance with its bodily constitution—arrives at a cognition of spiritual realities and finally comes to a cognition of God.[14] We see Jesus and recognize God. For He

[14] Cf. Thomas Aquinas, Summa theologiae III, q. 60.

says, "Whoever has seen me has seen the Father" (John 14:9) and "The Father and I are one" (John 10:30).

St. Augustine coherently conceptualizes the reciprocal mediation of truth in the God-Man, Jesus Christ:

> But since the [human] mind itself ... in this faith ... might advance the more confidently towards the truth, the truth itself, God, God's Son, assuming humanity without destroying His divinity, established and founded this faith, that there might be a way for man to man's God through a God-man. For this is the Mediator between God and men, the man Christ Jesus. For it is as man that He is the Mediator and the Way [1 Tim 2:5]. Since, if the way lies between him who goes, and the place whither he goes, there is hope of his reaching it; but if there be no way, or if he know not where it is, what boots it to know whither he should go? Now the only way that is infallibly secured against all mistakes is when the very same person is at once God and man, God our end, man our way.[15]

Supreme knowledge of God is enacted in the worship of God: "But the hour is coming, and is now here, when the true worshippers will worship the Father in spirit and truth, for the Father seeks such as these to worship him. God is spirit, and those who worship him must worship in spirit and truth" (John 4:23–24).

We hear Jesus' human voice and hear the Word of God that has been *light and life* from all eternity. When we accept God's Word in faith, it becomes our light and life as human beings (cf. John 1:4, 9). Thomas, putting his fingers into the wounds of

---

[15] Augustine, *De civ. Dei* XI, 2.

the transfigured body of Jesus, the Word who had become flesh, recognizes him as "my Lord and my God" (John 20:28). And one day, in heavenly glory, we shall see God face-to-face with our own eyes. We shall recognize Him through the sensitive and intelligible cognitive image of Christ's humanity and recognize how God lives and reigns in His triune love forever and ever.

Immanuel Kant (1724–1804), with his critical epistemology, could recognize God only as an idea of pure reason whose existence we are unable to verify. God, if He exists, would have no possibility of communicating Himself to us in the human word of the prophets and of Christ. We could never distinguish a real word of God from a product of our own imagination. Since the mind is able to assemble only what the senses present to it categorially into an image and concept (phenomenon) of our consciousness, what we cognize is merely the constructs of our thinking, not reality in its own being (the "thing in itself").

It has been said that Kant dug up the tree of knowledge, cut off its roots, and then rammed its pointed end back into the ground. No one will be surprised that no fruits of the knowledge of God and blissful love of Him were able to grow and ripen on its desiccated branches. But the human intellect or spirit is more than the operative mind. Rather, it is the reception room of being. The creation of the concepts of concrete language is preceded by the supra-conceptual intuition of being, providing us with evidence of the original grounds of being, which are also the principles of cognition and discursive thinking. To declare God to be an illusion and the product of wishful thinking is merely the eureka experience of the cat that keeps falling just short of its goal because, in constantly chasing round and round in circles, it fails to catch its own tail. To rule out God's existence because it does not meet the criteria of empiricism and positivism founders on the spiritual nature of God, who is identical with His own subsistent being and thus does not need any ideal and material ground of possibility for His existence. God exists through His own reality and not by virtue of the imagined possibility that our finite thinking ascribes to Him without ever being able to verify the real existence of ideas of pure reason or the postulates of practical, i.e., moral, reason.

The anti-Christian scheme of atheology with which the French popular philosopher Michel Onfray (b. 1959) wishes to get to the heart of modern criticism of religion is nothing more than a self-referential *petitio principii*.[16]

In the simile of being (*Gleichnis des Seins*), its transcendent ground becomes clear to us—namely, God as the origin, meaning, and goal of all that exists.[17] Our language is more than just a vegetative-animal system for communicating about food, reproduction, parental care, and the avoidance of danger. Why does the infant waste away whose ear never hears the loving words of a mother? Why is solitary confinement hell for us if we have no linguistic contact with fellow human beings? In language, man enacts his essence (*Wesen*) as the disclosedness (*Erschlossenheit*) of being and its knowability. Human beings do not merely inform others about the practical necessities for survival, but rather communicate themselves in language, so that a reciprocal disclosedness takes place from "I" to "I." Human beings are not just spatially present in the world like a monkey in a space capsule; they are

---

[16] Michel Onfray, *Traité d'athéologie. Physique de la métaphysique* (Paris: Grasset, 2005; English: *Atheist Manifesto: The Case against Christianity, Judaism, and Islam*, trans. Jeremy Leggatt (New York: Arcade, 2007).

[17] Gustav Siewerth, *Das Sein als Gleichnis Gottes: Gesammelte Werke I* (Düsseldorf: Patmos-Verlag, 1975), 651–697.

essentially spirit in the world.[18] "Language is the house of being. In its home human beings dwell. Those who think and those who create with words are the guardians of this home. Their guardianship accomplishes the manifestation of being insofar as they bring this manifestation to language and preserve it in language through their saying."[19]

This was put more primordially by John in his Gospel: "In the beginning was the Word, and the Word was with God, and the Word was God.... No one has ever seen God. It is God the only Son, who is close to the Father's heart, who has made him known" (John 1:1, 18). God's self-revelation exists only because God enacts His eternal being relationally in the begetting uttering of the Word and the loving spiration of the Spirit, who unites Father and Son in the depths of God's being. "For the Spirit searches everything, even the depths of God" (1 Cor. 2:10).

In Islam, God, according to His eternal essence, is not in Himself relational in word and spirit. This is why the Quran is not translatable: the message of God received by its human mediator does not already exist in God Himself as a *Wesenswort* (essence word) before its revelation. It exists uncreated in the dictated Arabic language and cannot be detached from it. Content and text are absolutely identical. The Bible, however, can be translated into every language since the Word of God, which is God Himself, can be understood through the prophets and finally in His

[18] Karl Rahner, *Geist in Welt. Zur Metaphysik der endlichen Erkenntnis bei Tomas von Aquin* [1936] (= KRSW 2, Freiburg i. Br., 1996, 3–300). English: *Spirit in the World* (New York: Herder, 1968).

[19] Martin Heidegger, *Brief über den Humanismus* (Frankfurt a. M.: Vittorio Klostermann, 1975), 5. English: *Letter on Humanism*, trans. Frank A. Capuzzi (1949), 239, Internet Archive, https://archive.org/details/heidegger-letter-on-humanism-capuzzi.

consubstantial Son (see Heb. 1:1–4) by every human mind in its mother tongue. This means that within the continuously identical faith community of the Church, the many nations, even though they understood neither Hebrew nor Aramaic nor Greek as categories, comprehended, as it were, transcendentally in the Holy Spirit the whole content of the apostles' preaching. But every language is, by virtue of the Holy Spirit, receptive to the word of the triune God, who thus enters into a personal dialogue with each individual human being. And so in the Son, we can call God Abba, Father, because the Holy Spirit of their mutual love has been poured into our hearts (see Rom 5:5; 8:15; Gal. 4:6).

Dissatisfied with the philosophically and theologically so multifaceted and infinitely profound meaning of *logos* being translated with the term *word*, Professor Faust toys with the concepts of *mind* (*Sinn, sensus*—also "thought" in various translations) and *power* (*Kraft, virtus*). Finally, a flash of inspiration comes to his aid. Remembering Johann Gottlieb Fichte (1762–1814), the philosopher of subjective idealism, he writes with satisfaction: "In the beginning was the *act* (*Tat*)." This radical reversal from the enunciating word to the "fact-act" (*Tathandlung*) is also an act of self-liberation from the typically German inwardness into which Lutheran Christianity had retreated. The world and history were once again to be a space where the divine, the absolute spirit is manifested. The frowned-upon righteousness that comes from good works that are rooted in grace had returned as a man-made New World without the prevenient grace that precedes everything we do.

After Immanuel Kant, the founder of critical idealism, had declared real being unknowable, thereby leaving only a knowledge of the phenomena that we ourselves produce, the idealism of Fichte, Schelling, and Hegel arrived at a construction of the world from the cognizing subject. Through our thoughts we speculatively build the world of our cognition, and through our deeds we create our moral world in autonomous freedom.

But modern subject philosophy, which since Descartes had sought the *fundamentum inconcussum* [firm foundation] in the consciousness of the thinking I, also foundered on the fact that our discursive, world-bound cognition cannot circumvent its conditionality and limitedness. It is a priori impossible for a finite mind, i.e., an intellect that knows itself to be conditioned in its being and in its acts of thinking, to found itself in its thinking as well as its being.

In its being and thinking, this mind is founded in something else that is not at its disposal but of which it may gratefully profess itself to be the image and participation. It understands itself in its finite thinking and contingent being as existing in a creaturely manner. No one can pull himself out of the mire by his own bootstraps. The finite, sensorially bound mind has no immediate evidence of the truth of being and of its own thinking self. Without Ariadne's thread—i.e., without the uncreated light—we shall never find our way out of the labyrinth of the confusing and contradictory impressions and constraints of world events. So if we cannot find the firm footing from which to lift the world off its hinges or fix it in place in the order of knowledge, could we then give the order of being a try? But being as such remains closed to us because it shows itself only in that which exists in a limited manner and at the same time eludes us. Somehow every finite and created intellect finds itself in a vicious circle from which we cannot escape by our own efforts. A self-founding in itself of thinking that is stuck in the finite is impossible. In free fall, I can save myself only if I can catch hold of something to grasp that is itself firmly anchored.

All thinking presupposes real and objective being; at the same time, being is cognized only through the conditions of the subject of cognition. But we cannot get behind the being of the world either, and we never have it present in its totality and depth in a single act of cognition. We are distracted, and it is only with the greatest effort that we succeed in getting to the heart of a single thought. We cannot go back empirically behind the initial conditions of the cosmos and fathom their logic through reflection. Since our finite reason can grasp nothingness only as a thought-thing, we cannot get to the beginning of finite, i.e., created, being through thinking either. For that would mean that we could adequately think God's being without being God ourselves. The *beginning* in which the Word was and the beginning in which God created Heaven and earth is therefore not the point on the line of time and the place in space where matter began to unfold into its present form. Time does not become a problem just for the cosmology of the sensorially objective world; it is already one for our unsecured existence in the contingency, the non-necessity, of our individual existence. Nor can God be thought by comparing Him to a successive sequence or to expanding relative and absolute space-time. We need a point of reference outside the subject-object structure of human cognition. And that is God, the Creator who freely communicates Himself to us because He is neither positively nor negatively dialectically mediated with the world in His being or in His self-knowledge and self-affirmation.

But our striving for Him in our reason and moral will arrives at its goal only when He makes Himself known to us in *His Word* and offers Himself to us to love in His *Spirit*. The knowledge of God in His Logos, which is reflected in the works of creation, and the knowledge of God in the logic of His self-revelation in the history of salvation achieve a synthesis in supernatural faith. This synthesis does not, however, offer any insight into a logical and real state of affairs but rather enables the encounter with the person of the divine Logos. As the Son of the Father, He bears in His Divine Person the unity of a divine and a human nature. The Logos meets us concretely—i.e., able to be seen, heard and touched—in Jesus of Nazareth, the Messiah of the Jews and the Savior of the whole world.

At the origins of the history of Western thought, the Greek philosophers searched for the first beginnings, causes, elements, and building materials of the cosmos and sought the principles and ideas that order and constitute it.

Six centuries before the Gospel of John, Heraclitus of Ephesus had, in his Fragment 1, already seen the eternal law of the world as being grounded in God's all-pervading reason, which unites the multiplicity of appearances and becomes recognizable in the agonal world process. The Logos surpasses all understanding, even if its existence is recognized in its effect (*Wirksamkeit*). The Logos, which is common to all human beings, also grounds man's relationship to the God-Logos and makes intellectual cognition and responsible moral action possible.

Modern science has not progressed much beyond ionic natural philosophy if no less a person than Albert Einstein (1879-1955) presents his worldview in such a way that, without any belief in a personal God and the immortality of the soul, he can say: "Enough for me the mystery of the eternity of life, and the inkling of the marvellous structure of reality, together with the single-hearted endeavour to comprehend a portion, be it never so tiny, of the reason that manifests itself in nature."[20]

Aristotle's metaphysics takes us a decisive step further toward understanding the Logos nature of God. "The God" is the unmoved

---

[20] Albert Einstein, *Mein Weltbild*, ed. Carl Selig (Zürich, 2019), 12. English: *The World as I See It* (London, 1935; rev. 2007), 5.

mover who does not realize Himself like the rest of the cosmos through His possibilities but is that which is (*das Seiende*) in pure reality. He is essentially intelligible and appropriates Himself (*ereignet sich*) eternally as the thinking of thinking. God is thinking being-at-one-with-Himself (*Bei-sich-sein*), supreme and unsurpassable intellectual presence, pure actual being.

This is the closest possible approximation of human reason to divine reason, which, however, utters itself in its historical revelation as Word and communicates itself to us as Person. The Word, which was with God in the beginning and which is God, is the connecting link between the philosophical logos, which we translate as "reason," and the Logos of God, which, on account of its self-revelation in Jesus Christ, we translate as "Word." The early Christian philosopher Justin Martyr (ca. AD 100–165) sees in every cognizing of the truth by the pre-Christian thinkers scattered sparks of the one divine light and the scattered seeds of the one Word of God, which came into the world in full measure in Jesus Christ.

The world, with all the material universes that we have perhaps not yet empirically established, is not just a cosmos that, in its demiurgically designed order, has been wrested from chaos. Rather, the world is God's creation because it came into being through the Logos, the Divine Person of the Son, and because nothing came into being without the Word. Hence, its logical structure is the expression of its recognizability as participation in God's eternal knowing Himself (*Sich-Selbst-Erkennen*) in the Logos and eternal willing or wanting himself (*Sich-Selbstwollen*) in the Spirit of the mutual love between Father and Son. What is invisible about God—namely, His eternal power and divinity—is known by us through reason. But reason is wise and insightful only if we also honor God with our free will and show Him gratitude. Only

when we worship God the Creator alone and do not idolize creatures instead of Him and in our own bodies fall into dishonorable
relationships and sins (see Rom. 1:18–32) are we not at the mercy
of the "powers and principalities" (Eph. 6:12).

Understanding the becoming of all creation in the Logos is
something quite different from theologizing cosmology. Ludwig
Wittgenstein (1889–1951), as a representative of the analytical
philosophy of language, emphasizes the difference between philosophical thinking and natural science. Man's relationship to God
is not categorially determined by space and time but by man's
constitution as a person, so that his existence in space and time is
enfolded in his relationship to the eternal God. So Wittgenstein
states: "If by eternity is understood not endless temporal duration
but timelessness, then he lives eternally who lives in the *present*. Our
life is endless in the way that our visual field is without limit."[21]
One would like to add: man lives in the presence of God in relation to God's being as pure reality.

"*How* the world is, is completely indifferent for what is higher.
God does not reveal himself *in* the world."[22] "Not *how* the world
is, is the mystical, but *that* it is."[23]

Creatureliness does not mean for man only that God is an
external cause that is part of the finite being that is to be explained
and itself again needs a cause. God, in His will toward the singular
objects existing as creatures, is the act through which being makes

---

[21] Ludwig Wittgenstein, *Tractatus logico-philosophicus* 6.4311, ed. J.
Schulte (Frankfurt a. M., 2019), 109. English: *Tractatus Logico-
Philosophicus*, trans. C. K. Ogden (London: Kegan Paul, Trench,
Trubner, 1922), Project Gutenberg, https://www.gutenberg.org/
ebooks/5740.

[22] Ibid., 6.432.

[23] Ibid., 6.44.

possible the subsistence of that which is (*actus essendi*). He is the transcendent principle of their existence. The triune God is the origin, content, and goal of my whole existence in experienced time and hoped-for eternity. God "chose us in Christ before the foundation of the world" (Eph. 1:4). The "God and Father of our Lord Jesus Christ … destined us for adoption as his children through Jesus Christ, according to the good pleasure of his will" (Eph. 1:3, 5). Man, as person in reason and will, exists through the act of being borne by God. Man lives in Him and toward Him. The "word of life" (1 John 1:1) that the apostolic "servants of the word" (Luke 1:2) have to proclaim to us is "the eternal life that was with the Father and was revealed to us" (1 John 1:2). Mediated through the sacramental community of the Church, "truly our fellowship is with the Father and with his Son Jesus Christ" (1 John 1:3). "By this we know that we abide in him and he in us, because he has given us of his Spirit" (1 John 4:13).

In the beginning, before all time and beyond the spread of any matter in space, was the eternal Word, and the Word was with God and God was the Word. "In him was life, and the life was the light of all people" (John 1:4).

With respect to the presence of God in His Logos and Pneuma, we comprehend that omnipresence, omniscience, and omnipotence are not only essential attributes of God in His nature but are characteristics shared by the three Divine Persons.

The fact that God is the Logos in the Person of the "only Son of the Father" (see John 1:18; 2 John 3) means that God is really present to Himself in the full thinking and willing self-ownership of His divinity. The world exists as participation in God's knowledge of Himself (in the Word) and resolve (*Entschlossenheit*) to Himself (in the Spirit). And that is the foundation upon which rests His real presence in the world, His creation, through the same Logos who assumed our flesh from the Virgin Mary. "But to all who received him, who believed in his name, he gave power to become children of God, who were born, not of blood or of the will of the flesh or of the will of man, but of God" (John 1:12–13).

Chapter 2

And the Word became flesh

John 1:14

"And the Word became flesh": this is the truth of all truths, the focus and foundation of the Christian faith. He who created us in our flesh and blood also redeems us in our flesh, which He made His own flesh and blood. God is in the world in the scandalous form of flesh. This is the contradiction that He Himself presents to the idealistic God as an idea or cipher for the improvement of the world. Christianity cannot be made digestible to the world so that it suits its tastes. It is neither an NGO nor a propaganda office for the creation of the New Man and an ideal world order.

Belief in the God in the flesh forms the eschatological dividing line between Christ and the antichrist. "Every spirit that confesses that Jesus Christ has come in the flesh is from God, and every spirit that does not confess Jesus is not from God. And this is the spirit of the antichrist" (1 John 4:2–3).

God is not only intentionally close to us as spirit and truth but is present in our corporeal-spiritual nature, in every dimension of our worldliness. Each of you, look at yourself in your corporeality. Hold your hand in front of your eyes and understand that present in your passible and corruptible flesh is the One who created you for life and redeemed you from death. This is the

God's Presence in the Eucharist and in the World

God beside whom there is no other God because the Absolute and Holy cannot be divided among several subjects without losing its absoluteness and infiniteness. Look at your brothers in front of you and beside you. And make yourself aware that your Savior lived on earth in the same human flesh and blood that constitute the bodily existence of your neighbor. Only then can we also understand the words of the Son of Man when He comes in glory with all His angels and says to us from the throne of His divinity: "Truly, I say to you, as you did it to one of the least of these my brethren, you did it to me" and, likewise referring to having seen them hungry and thirsty, "Truly, I say to you, as you did it not to one of the least of these, you did it not to me" (Matt. 25:40, 45, RSVCE).

Through Baptism we become members of the Body of Christ. And through our incorporation into the Body of Christ, we are children of God and temples of the Holy Spirit. By eating the Eucharistic bread, we share in the Body of Christ, which was born of Mary and is now in the transfigured form of the risen Lord at the right hand of the Father in Heaven. When we drink from the "cup of blessing" (1 Cor. 10:16) at Holy Mass, we now share in the Blood of Christ, which He shed historically once for all on the altar of the Cross for the salvation of the world.

God in my flesh! This is the truth that no created mind could ever conceive. It surpasses anything we could have hoped for from God, even in our wildest dreams. God "in the likeness of sinful flesh" (Rom. 8:3) is a scandal to all reason, which, although conscious of its own limitations, nevertheless declares itself the measure of all that is real and possible. The God on the Cross in the flesh of His Son flies in the face of the complacent wisdom of this world. And that is why God decided "through the foolishness of our proclamation, to save those who believe" (1 Cor. 1:21). It is not just reason that blinds the proud but also sin, preventing them from recognizing the Logos through whom the world came into being. For the world came into being through the Logos of God, and "to all who received him, who believed in his name, he gave power to become children of God" (John 1:12). We are children of God in recognizing the Father in the Son and loving God in the Spirit of the Father and the Son.

Thus, the finite reason with which the God-Logos endowed us faces a unique challenge. On the one hand, the Incarnation of the Logos cannot be deduced from the possibilities of human thought, but on the other hand, our reason achieves its supreme realization when, in the light of faith, it receives a share in the uncreated reason of God and when we recognize God in Christ as He recognizes Himself in His Essence Word (*Wesens-Wort*). "For the Spirit searches everything, even the depths of God. For what human being knows what is truly human except the human spirit that is within? So also no one comprehends what is truly God's except the Spirit of God. Now we have received not the spirit of the world, but the Spirit that is from God, so that we may understand the gifts bestowed on us by God" (1 Cor. 2:10–12). After the resurrection of the flesh, "I will know fully, even as I have been fully known" (1 Cor. 13:12).

But we do not want to signal the superiority of Christian knowledge of the Incarnation by putting ourselves above the philosophies (Neo-Platonism and transcendental philosophy) and the other monotheistic religions (Islam, postbiblical Judaism) that consider the Incarnation to be completely incompatible with God's absolute transcendence. For with Christ it is not just a new idea that has entered the history of ideas but rather the absolute novelty that He Himself is in His Divine Person in freely assuming our human nature—as Irenaeus elaborated against Gnosticism.[24] The revelation of God in Christ comes to us through the supernatural light of the Holy Spirit as we surrender ourselves to God in the "obedience of faith" (Rom. 1:5; 16:26; 2 Cor. 10:5–6). Gratitude toward grace does not permit self-glory that exalts itself above fellow human beings who are still journeying toward "the knowledge of the glory of God in the face of Jesus Christ" (2 Cor. 4:6).

We only need to think of the axiom of Apuleius of Madaurus in the second century: "Between God and man there is no possibility of contact."[25]

No one before or after Christ has ever claimed that the Absolute has entered time, that the Creator of Heaven and earth Himself has become a part of the world and that the Lord over history has made Himself an active agent and a passive plaything of the contingency of finite freedom. The profession of "God in our flesh" is regarded by idealists as a megalomaniacal blasphemy and by materialists as a relapse into foolish mythologies and prescientific thinking. But we Christians do not believe in a deified human being or in a mythological God in human disguise. Our belief in Christ the God-Man is therefore not a religious symbol, not a metaphysical speculation, and not mythological poetry.

Against this stands Jesus' self-testimony that the Word who is God Himself took on our flesh. We believe in the Son of God who became man so that we might share in His divine life. Our faith is therefore based not on prior hypotheses about what is possible and probable but rather on Jesus' own self-testimony: "I came from the Father and have come into the world; again, I am leaving the world and am going to the Father" (John 16:28). Only in the light

[24] Irenaeus of Lyon, *Adversus haereses* IV, 34, 1.
[25] Apuleius, *De Deo Socratis* 4, 128.

of Jesus' self-testimony do we, with the aid of grace, come to profess: Jesus is the Lord, the Son of the Father, the Word made flesh, the Second Person of the Trinity. The Church's doctrine confesses with the Fathers of the Council of Chalcedon (451) the Incarnation of the Logos as the undivided and unmixed union of the divine and human natures of Jesus Christ in the Divine Person of the Word:

> Following therefore the holy Fathers, we unanimously teach to confess one and the same Son, our Lord Jesus Christ, the same perfect in divinity and perfect in humanity, the same truly God and truly one man composed of rational soul and body, the same one in being with the Father as to the divinity and one in being with us as to the humanity, like unto us in all things but sin. The same was begotten from the Father before the ages as to the divinity and in the latter days for us and for our salvation was born as to his humanity from Mary the Virgin Mother of God.
>
> [We confess that] one and the same Lord Jesus Christ, the only begotten Son, must be acknowledged in two natures, without confusion or change, without division or separation. The distinction between the natures was never abolished by their union but rather the character proper to each of the two natures was preserved as they came together in one Person and one hypostasis. He is not split or divided into two Persons, but he is one and the same only begotten Son, God the Word [Logos], the Lord Jesus Christ, as formerly the prophets and later Jesus Christ himself have taught us about him and has been handed down to us by the creed of the Fathers.[26]

---

[26] DH 301–302.

God's Presence in the Eucharist and in the World

A historical reconstruction and literary analysis of the biblical texts will only lead us to the conceptualization and the mode of expression of the Apostles' Creed but not to the supernatural act of my personal and free assent to the truth of God that is uttered in the human words of Jesus and realized historically, once and for all, in His life, death, and Resurrection from the dead.

For the whole Church of all times, Simon Peter answers Jesus' question as to whether we, too, want to go away: "Lord, to whom can we go? You have the words of eternal life. We have come to believe and know that you are the Holy One of God" (John 6:68-69). "We" here refers to the disciples of Jesus, not the "Jews," i.e., the members of God's covenant people who took offense at Him because He wanted to give us His flesh to eat. But the faith of Jesus' disciples—who were "first called Christians" at Antioch (Acts 11:26)—is also being put to the test today.

Albert Schweitzer, in his groundbreaking work *The Quest for the Historical Jesus* (*Die Geschichte der Leben-Jesu-Forschung*, 1906) attests that every procedure attempting to produce a historical reconstruction of the life of Jesus has failed. It is not possible, he concludes, for Jesus to be brought into our time. All that is left to us is to have a mystical relationship with Jesus in which we let ourselves be inspired or enchanted by His wonderful personality. But since this rationalist thinking has only the historicist category available to it, there can be no ecclesial and sacramental mediation through which the Lord, dwelling as He does with the Father, makes Himself really present in the Holy Spirit both in the words of preaching and profession and in the sacraments and community of the Church.

The New Testament in no way contains a variety of theological constructs that are linked to some so-called existential significance of Jesus. It is always concerned with the mystery of the Person of Jesus. Only in the revealed faith do we recognize Him as the Son of the Father, who in His Divine Word expresses Himself *eternally* in the divinity of Christ and presents Himself *temporally* in the human nature that He assumed from Mary. The Gospel of John starts with the Divine Person of the Word and unfolds this mystery in the historical self-interpretation in the human nature of Christ. The Synoptic Gospels, on the other hand, lead us through the human history of Jesus to a knowledge of His oneness with the Father, whose Son and Revealer He is. In what is the key hermeneutical passage for synoptic Christology, Jesus testifies to Himself in His divine origin and mission: "Yes, Father, for such was your gracious will. All things have been handed over to me by my Father; and no one knows the Son except the Father, and no one knows the Father except the Son and anyone to whom the Son chooses to reveal him" (Matt. 11:26–27; cf. Luke 10:21–22).

And this is the premise: namely, that Jesus' "Father in heaven" revealed the personal mystery of Jesus to Simon Peter. God's Trinitarian self-revelation is therefore the origin, foundation, and expression of the Church's profession of Jesus, her Lord and Head: "You are the Christ, the Son of the living God" (Matt. 16:16). God's self-revelation in the testimony of the Son for the Father and of the Father for the Son renders it impossible still to speak of God without Christ (*remoto Christo*) and, apart from the witnessing community, the Church, to form an image of Jesus according to one's own taste (e.g., Jesus as the ideal of the educated citizen, the first socialist, the conservationist and environmental activist, etc.). For it is true: "Those who believe in the Son of God have the testimony in their hearts. Those who do not believe in God have made him a liar by not believing in the testimony that God has given concerning his Son" (1 John 5:10).

Only when the supernatural faith infused into our hearts enables us to know the truth that the Word who is God took on flesh and dwells among us does it also become clear to us that Jesus is the Emmanuel, the God-with-us (see Matt. 1:23). Then we are built up by His promise that whenever His disciples are gathered together, be it in a large or small gathering, He will remain among them (see Matt. 18:20), which is, after all, what is meant by His assurance "And remember, I am with you always, to the end of the age" (Matt. 28:20).

Jesus as a man is "the way" and as God "the truth and the life" (John 14:6). We walk the spiritual path of following Christ, the aim of which is to lead us to knowing God in the face of Christ (see 2 Cor. 4:6). We are mystically conformed to Christ in an inner process of purification, enlightenment, and union. We are called and are children of God (see 1 John 3:1). We are adopted in Christ as sons and daughters of God who confidently call out to God: "Abba, Father" (see Gal. 4:6; Rom. 8:15) "because God's love has been poured into our hearts through the Holy Spirit that has been given to us" (Rom. 5:5).

Chapter 3

Let there be light

Genesis 1:3

For us, the Sacred Scriptures of the Old and New Testaments are not a book of pious edification or layers of sunken sediments from the analysis of which archaeologists can obtain the material for their historical reconstructions. The Bible is and contains the word of the living God. God speaks really and relevantly to us. The triune God — the Father and the Son, and the Holy Spirit — communicates Himself in the manner of a dialogue to His chosen covenant people and eschatologically to all humankind. He reveals Himself as the purpose and goal of all creation, as the Judge and Savior of every individual human being (see Matt. 28:19). The historical-critical method analyzes only the fashion in which God's word is communicated, i.e., the shape it takes in human language (grammar and syntax) and in human thought (the first philosophy or metaphysics of the principles of being and cognition, the rules of logic, the categories of understanding and the conceptualization of a mind that always starts with sensory perception).

Sacred Scripture is God's word in human language (see 1 Thess. 2:13). It is the fundamental document in which the testimony of the prophets and the preaching of the apostles are, as it were, an inexhaustible source feeding the living tradition of the Church as expressed in the form of her Creed and liturgy. But just as the hypostatic—i.e., personal—union of the divine and human natures in Christ prevents us from separating the one Divine Word of the Son of God from the many human words of Jesus, we cannot separate the word of God from the definitive literary shape it takes in the Bible either. Dogmatic and historical interpretation can be distinguished methodologically, but they cannot be separated in the act of faith as this is directed toward the God-Man, Jesus Christ. The believer's act is directed toward the proclaimed truth. The (grammatical, literary, cultural-historical) manner in which it is expressed serves as its medium so as to arrive at a knowledge of the First and Uncreated Truth, which is God Himself in His Word-Logos eternally and temporally expressing itself and in His Spirit bestowing itself from the Father and the Son—as is stated by Thomas Aquinas.[27] Jesus rose from the dead; His body is no longer historically visible here on earth. But He lives in His transfigured humanity with the Father and *remains with us* with His assumed human nature through word and sacrament—remaining with His disciples always to the end of the age (see Matt. 28:20; John 15:4). For this reason, the written testimony of the apostolic faith cannot be dissected like a corpse from history in the delusion that we can bring it back to life in our subjective imagination. Christ, "who was raised, who is at the right hand of God, who indeed intercedes for us" (Rom. 8:34), is present only as a fiction in the

---

[27] Thomas Aquinas, *Summa theologiae* II-II, q. 1, a. 2, ad 2: "Actus autem credentis non terminatur ad enuntiabile, sed ad rem: non enim formamus enuntiabilia nisi ut per ea de rebus cognitionem habeamus, sicut in scientia, ita et in fide. ["Now the act of the believer does not terminate in a proposition, but in a thing. For as in science we do not form propositions, except in order to have knowledge about things through their means, so is it in faith."]

Hollywood films about Jesus; but in the tabernacles on the altars of His Church, His presence is real.

In Sacred Scripture, we read in the Holy Spirit the witness of God's people to the history of their encounter with God. God has progressively spoken Himself into the faith consciousness of Israel and the Church and thus written Himself into their faith documents. In this sense, He Himself is the actual author of the "sacred writings," for all "scripture is inspired by God" (2 Tim. 3:15-16). For it is God Himself who "[has spoken] to our ancestors in many and various ways by the prophets, but in these last days he has spoken to us by a Son" (Heb. 1:1-2). So in the Old Testament, Christ was present in a hidden way, while in the New Testament, the promise of universal salvation became flesh in the Son of God.[28] Ultimately, the unity of the self-revelation in the testimony of the Old and New Testaments can also be recognized, in both reason and faith, on the historical and literary level because it presupposes the unity of Father and Son in the Holy Spirit and reveals their unity in *Word* and *Spirit*.

Because the living God is the subject of His self-revelation in word and deed, hearing His word and reading the testimonies of His historical revelation also generates faith in God in the spirit. Believers who are enlightened in the Holy Spirit do not stop at a simple encounter with the dead letter. Rather, they come to understand its meaning in the Holy Spirit. " 'The word is near you,

---

[28] Cf. Augustine, *Questiones in Heptateuchum* 2, 73: "Multum et solide significatur ad vetus testamentum timorem potius pertinere sicut ad novum dilectionem, quamquam et in vetere novum lateat et in novo vetus pateat. ["This passage signifies a great and lasting truth: that fear pertains to the Old Testament just as love does to the New—even though the New lies hidden in the Old Testament, and the Old Testament is opened up in the New."]

on your lips and in your heart' (that is, the word of faith that we proclaim); because if you confess with your lips that *Jesus is Lord* and believe in your heart that *God raised him from the dead*, you will be saved" (Rom. 10:8-9).

> These things [the mystery of his wisdom] God has revealed to us through the Spirit; for the Spirit searches everything, even the depths of God.... Now we have received not the spirit of the world, but the Spirit that is from God, so that we may understand the gifts bestowed on us by God.... Those who are unspiritual [i.e., rationalists and positivists] do not receive the gifts of God's Spirit, for they are foolishness to them, and they are unable to understand them because they are discerned spiritually. Those who are spiritual discern all things, and they are themselves subject to no one else's scrutiny. (1 Cor. 2:10-15)

So for those who believe in God in Christ, the Bible is the dogmatic foundation of the Creed, the effervescent source of spiritual life, and the moral orientation for how they live their lives. The dogmatic—i.e., canonical—and the historical-critical interpretation of the Bible go hand in hand. *Lectio divina* recognizes the spirit in the letter. Historical-critical exegesis sees in the historical form of revelation the flesh that the divine Logos assumed in Jesus Christ.

On opening the Bible, we already encounter the concept of *beginning* in the Old Testament and then seen with John's eagle eye in the prologue to his Gospel. It refers not to the time of the beginning of all that is created but rather to the origin of time in the present eternity of God. In the beginningless beginning, the Word was with God as the Word that is God Himself. And in the Word all things were created (see John 1:1). In the Word made flesh, the eternal procession of the Son from the Father is thus revealed as the origin and goal of all creation, in particular man's eternal calling to be a child of God in Christ and a friend of God in the Holy Spirit. "He destined us for adoption as his children through Jesus Christ, according to the good pleasure of his will, to the praise of his glorious grace" (Eph. 1:5-6).

So over the existence of the whole world and its history stands the original confession (*Urbekenntnis*) of the Church: "In the beginning God … created the heavens and the earth" (Gen. 1:1). Even though there seemed to be a balance between chaos and the cosmos before the works of differentiation and embellishment, creation was still never able to escape God's preserving and ordering omnipotence. For God's Spirit, with His creative omnipotence, hovered in a calming and stabilizing way over the primordial flood and did not allow the nihilating nothingness the slightest chance. The fact of being created in the contingency of everything that is finite does not fill us with fear but rather generates in us a reaction of creaturely joy, the eucharistic sense of gratitude and free obedience to the gracious and merciful God. The power of death and evil is not only historically and factually vanquished by Christ but is also swallowed up from all eternity by God's life and goodness.

Any form of dualism is a priori incompatible with the Christian belief in God, the Creator of the whole universe. This applies to Plato's idealistic dualism with its separation of being into an invisible and a visible world. And it applies even more to the moral dualism of Marcion and the Manichaeans, who assumed two antagonistic absolute principles of good and evil. They framed this in the theory of the supposed contradiction between an Old Testament God of vengeance and a New Testament God of love, or that of the dialectical contradiction between an evil Creator God and a good Redeemer God. Since the beginning of modern subject philosophy, the role played by the anthropological dualism of René Descartes (1596–1650) is not to be underestimated. The two independent substances of consciousness and body, *res cogitans et res extensa*, are only accidentally connected at all in man and in reality. Here man is not a substantial unity of two dependent components of the spiritual soul (*Geistseele*) and the body it animates; rather, he is an accidental unity of two complete substances, each of which subsists in itself, thus bursting the unity of the individual in his or her personhood in which the composite of body and soul subsists. Man is person in his current consciousness and only resides in his body as in a container. It is only such an understanding that makes possible the idea of gender reassignment, i.e., the notion that we could acquire a different body because, as a man or a woman, we feel as if we are in the body of the wrong gender. In the conflict between idealistic and materialistic monism, this dualistic approach blocked the whole of modern philosophy and theology and alienated many of its adherents from the knowledge of God in His historical and incarnational and sacramental presence. God becomes worldless, and the world becomes godless. Either God is spiritualistically imagined to be completely beyond the world and being, or He is fanatically denied for the sake of the autonomy of the world. But in the light of the world, we recognize the existence of God because He is its source.

John Henry Newman (1801–1890) overcame his youthful crisis of faith after reading Thomas Paine's polemic against the Old Testament, David Hume's essays on skeptical empiricism, and Voltaire's treatise against the immortality of the soul when, during his life-threatening illness on a trip to Sicily, he realized: "I shall not die, for I have not sinned against light."[29]

---

[29] Günter Biemer, *Die Wahrheit wird stärker sein. Das Leben Kardinal Newmans* (Wiesbaden: Peter Lang, 2002), 94.

On his journey back to England, he wrote this wonderful prayer:

> Lead, Kindly Light, amidst th'encircling gloom,
> Lead Thou me on!
> The night is dark, and I am far from home,
> Lead Thou me on!
> Keep Thou my feet; I do not ask to see
> The distant scene; one step enough for me.
>
> I was not ever thus, nor prayed that Thou
> Shouldst lead me on;
> I loved to choose and see my path; but now
> Lead Thou me on!
> I loved the garish day, and, spite of fears,
> Pride ruled my will. Remember not past years!
>
> So long Thy power hath blest me, sure it still
> Will lead me on.
> O'er moor and fen, o'er crag and torrent, till
> The night is gone,
> And with the morn those angel faces smile,
> Which I have loved long since, and lost awhile![30]

The inscription on his tombstone shows the path of human thinking that allows itself to be guided by God's light:

Ex umbris et imaginibus in veritatem[31]

The becoming of the light that initiates all being and cognition before, above, and in all creation, also rules out the double-truth

---

[30] John Henry Newman, written in 1833 and first published in the *British Magazine* in 1834 as "The Pillar of the Cloud" (= *Apologia pro Vita Sua*, pt. 3).

[31] Biemer, *Die Wahrheit wird stärker sein*, 94.

theory *a limine*. There is only the one created light that illuminates the reason of rational beings (angels and human beings). Human reason shares in the uncreated light of God, so that all truth recognized by anyone is truth that comes from God and leads toward truth. "Every truth by whomsoever spoken is from the Holy Ghost as bestowing the natural light, and moving us to understand and speak the truth, but not as dwelling in us by sanctifying grace, or as bestowing any habitual gift superadded to nature."[32]

The first words that issue from the mouth of God are that mighty command that ordains all being to be a reflection of God's reason, in which He eternally recognizes Himself: "Let there be light" (Gen. 1:3). These mighty words, which call forth both shivers and ecstasy, were set to music by Joseph Haydn (1732–1809)— with Mozart and Beethoven, one of the triumvirate of Viennese classicism—in his oratorio *The Creation*, in which he gives spectacularly powerful musical expression to the creative coming into being of the light.

The parallel shape of Genesis 1 and John 1 is unmistakable. The entire Faith of the Church regarding creation is summarized in the statement: "All things came into being through him, and without him not one thing came into being. What has come into being in him was life, and the life was the light of all people" (John 1:3–4). The graphic depiction of the work of creation in seven days and the story of the Garden of Eden are merely an analytical assessment to explicate the multiplicity of predicates that are already contained in the subject of the simple statement of faith.

I recall a discussion from my youth. As a budding theology student, I met up with some socially minded contemporaries at the barber's. They thought they could make a mockery of the

---

[32] Thomas Aquinas, *Summa theologiae* I-II, q. 109, a. 1, ad 1.

Faith by exposing the contradiction between the creation of light on the first day of creation and the creation of the sun and moon as sources of light on the third. But the biblical accounts of creation are, in accordance with their literary genre, neither empirical astrophysics nor mythological cosmogony. All its cosmological insights and historical events are interpreted, irrespective of the state of development of the empirical sciences, within the horizon of belief in God as the origin and goal of rational man, for whose sake the world exists.

Hence, the light that spreads out over all creation at the beginning does not refer to the electromagnetic waves that are measurable with the help of physics, chemistry, and biology; nor does it raise questions regarding the speed of light, the theory of relativity and quantum physics, or the big bang and the speed at which the universe is expanding. What "light" refers to here is the universal cognizability of all created things both in their material existence (*Bestand*) and in their individual ground of being as well as in their metaphysical principles of being and cognition. Matter, too, can be analyzed in its structures and modes of action only because it is recognizable through the essential form (*Wesensform*) that constitutes the concretely existing thing (the *intelligibile in sensibili*). The light we are talking about here is therefore the en-lightening horizon within in which natural reason operates. But it also means the light of grace of the Spirit of truth and revelation. Hence the prayer of the Apostle: "I pray that the God of our Lord Jesus Christ, the Father of glory, may give you a spirit of wisdom and revelation … so that, with the eyes of your heart enlightened, you may know what is the hope to which he has called you" (Eph. 1:17–18). We thank God for the physical eyesight of our bodies and the natural light of reason (*lumen naturale*) in which we recognize "his eternal power and divine nature … through the things he has made" (Rom. 1:20).

God's Presence in the Eucharist and in the World

Our natural reason would be an empty faculty if the world were not intelligible in itself. *Omne ens est verum.* The dynamic of our will toward the good and being united with it in love would come to nothing if the light above and in all creation were not one with the good. *Omne ens est verum.* "And God saw that the light was good" (Gen. 1:4).

Everything that has been created is, in principle, transparent in its existence and its essence, even though there are still so many dark holes in our knowledge of the structure of matter and the way it works and despite the fact that our knowledge of the world has, as yet anyway, progressed only as far as the first few centimeters of a snail in a hundred-meter race. But our real individual and collective cognizing, too, will always remain "piecemeal" in the fields of philosophy and the human and historical sciences during our earthly pilgrimage and will never get beyond seeing "in a mirror, dimly" (1 Cor. 13:12). But in principle, there can be no contradiction between the insights of the natural sciences and the knowledge of God in His supernatural revelation. For knowledge that comes from the word of God in faith shares in the infallibility of God, who reveals Himself in his *Wesens-Wort* (essence Word) and who is in Himself the truth. Only the Word who became flesh can say of Himself: "I am the truth" (John 14:6). Christ is the truth in person. The world's knowledge, on the other hand, is fallible (falsifiable) and always—with a healthy skepticism—capable of being corrected and supplemented. An apparent contradiction between the knowledge of truth coming from revelation and the knowledge derived from the created world arises only out of a false understanding of created things or an inadequate interpretation of them. Nevertheless, the insights from revelation and the findings of the natural sciences are not unrelated to each other. In theology, the analogy of the natural cognition of truth has to be taken into account. The better informed we are in philosophical, worldly knowledge, the better theology will fulfill its task of expounding the inner grounds of the reason of faith—even though the faith infused by the Holy Spirit cannot be deduced by the powers and insights of natural reason: "It is, therefore, evident that the opinion is false of those who asserted that it made no difference to the truth of the faith what anyone holds about creatures, so long as one thinks rightly about God.... For error concerning creatures ... spills over into false opinion about God, and takes men's minds away from Him, to whom faith seeks to lead them."[33]

But we also thank God for the capacity to distinguish between good and evil by virtue of the natural moral law, which we perceive in the moral discernment of our conscience as the voice of God (see Rom. 2:14-15). We thank God for the infused light of faith (*lumen fidei*) by being able to say through the Holy Spirit: "Jesus is Lord" (1 Cor. 12:3) and when we kneel before the risen Christ with the apostle Thomas and confess: "My Lord and my God" (John 20:28). We thank God for the "light of glory" in which we shall one day "see face to face" (1 Cor. 13:12).

In Christ, the uncreated light of eternal divine reason and the created light in which we recognize the true and living God as the origin and goal of all being are united.

"God is light and in him there is no darkness at all" (1 John 1:5). And He promises us the Messianic bringer of salvation: "I will give you as a light to the nations, that my salvation may reach to the end of the earth" (Isa. 49:6).

God makes him into "a covenant to the people, a light to the nations" (Isa. 42:6). Jesus Christ is the Word made flesh who was

---

[33] Thomas Aquinas, *Summa contra gentiles* II, chap. 3 (New York: Image Books, 1955).

with God in the eternal beginning before all temporal beginning and in whom the Father said, "Let there be light" (Gen. 1:3). The Word, the *Intellectus Divinus*, is the life and light of humankind. The light of the Logos shines in the darkness (see John 1:5). "But to all who received him, who believed in his name, he gave power to become children of God" (John 1:12). "It is God the only Son, who is close to the Father's heart, who has made him known" (John 1:18). The *Verbum Incarnatum* through whom grace and truth came, Jesus Christ, reveals Himself to His disciples in every age: "I am the light of the world. Whoever follows me will never walk in darkness but will have the light of life" (John 8:12).

Chapter 4

Let us make man

Genesis 1:26

The *first* words that God spoke, according to the account of His seven-day work of creation, were: "Let there be light" (Gen. 1:13). The *last* words "in the beginning" of all creation with which he concluded were: "Let us make man in our image, after our likeness" (Gen. 1:26, RSVCE). God thus revealed Himself to us human beings in His word as the origin of all creation and Himself as man's purpose and goal. The world does not come into being when God limits Himself in order to give us space. There is no dialectic of being and nothingness, of an abstract emptiness of the concept that would first have to pass through the process of contradiction in order to mediate itself processually into its totality. That would be an unchristian concept of a mutual contingency of the finiteness of our existence and the infinity of God. We would end up with Hegel's description of the "religion of the new age": "God himself is dead."[34] Man is not a puppet, a transient element of the absolute spirit that constitutes itself as it passes through world history and cancels out everything in it. The supreme gift that God has bestowed on His creatures is not just being, albeit

---

[34] Georg W. F. Hegel, *Glauben und Wissen* [1802/3] (= PhB 62b, Hamburg 1962, 124).

in the limited form of our human nature (*Wesen*), but rather His gift of subsistence, personal autonomy. As persons, we exist independently, uniquely, unrepeatably, and with full dignity and accountability before God. Only a spiritual nature is immediately related to God.[35]

So we are neither created into nothingness as into an empty space nor merely held above the abyss by the hand of a potentate who, in an act of sheer arbitrariness, could just as easily drop us again. To think in this way is consistent with the nominalistic fiction of the arbitrary God who had to secure His freedom through His unpredictability. We certainly cannot calculate God *more geometrico*, but we can rely on Him completely because faithfulness is the revelation of His nature as goodness. God's sovereignty consists in the fact that He gains nothing and loses nothing with Creation. In setting a creaturely mind and will vis-à-vis Himself in us humans, God is not acting out of a need to be loved by us but rather out of His inexhaustible and unincreasable goodness, which He communicates to us in such a way that we are permitted to share in the community of love between Father and Son and to participate in its reciprocity in the Holy Spirit for all eternity.

Every individual human being exists within the framework of his spiritual-bodily nature insofar as God gives him a share in His being through the *actus essendi*. For we have come to be through the Word, which He Himself is in all eternity. For this reason, too, we were chosen and predestined to be sons and daughters of God from all eternity—that is, even before time began. Therefore, man

---

[35] Thomas Aquinas, *Summa theologiae* II-II, q. 2, a. 3: "The rational nature, in as much as it apprehends the universal notion of good and being, is immediately related to the universal principle of being."

does not first exist and then, secondarily, receive a destiny in addition to his *ratio essendi*. Rather, the act of creation is the revelation of God's eternal salvific will toward us in time and history. The universal salvific will of God, "who desires everyone to be saved and to come to the knowledge of the truth" (1 Tim. 2:4), is thus grounded in God's eternal word and will toward Himself. This is clear to us because the mediator of creation and of historical salvation is one and the same person in Christ, the eternal Son of the Father. The Creator-God breathed His life-giving Spirit into our nostrils so that we became living flesh (see Gen. 2:7). "For he created all things so that they might exist; the generative forces [creatures] of the world are wholesome, and there is no destructive poison in them, and the dominion of Hades is not on earth. For righteousness is immortal" (Wisd. 1:14-15). Despite the infinite difference that God Himself is in relation to us, we human beings are not His playthings, puppets, or slaves; rather, we stand in a personal relationship as His partners, children, and friends. Through Christ we "have access in one Spirit to the Father. So then you are no longer strangers and aliens, but you are citizens with the saints and also members of the household of God" (Eph. 2:18-19). We are therefore not subjects but free citizens in the kingdom of God—the *Civitas Dei*.

So we know why we are on earth and where the path of our earthly pilgrimage leads us. The first and last words with which we thank God for our whole life and for having been created cannot be put better than in the formulation attempted by St. Augustine in his *Confessions*:

> Great art Thou, O Lord, and greatly to be praised; great
> is Thy power, and Thy wisdom infinite. And Thee would
> man praise; man, but a particle of Thy creation; man, that

bears about him his mortality, the witness of his sin, the witness that Thou resistest the proud: yet would man praise Thee; he, but a particle of Thy creation. Thou awakest us to delight in Thy praise; for Thou madest us for Thyself, and our heart is restless, until it repose in Thee — *Tu excitas, ut laudare te delectet, quia fecisti nos ad te et inquietum est cor nostrum, donec requiescat in te.*[36]

Man owes his unique position in the whole universe to God, who created man in His own image and likeness. It is no overestimation of our role if we understand ourselves as the beings for whose sake the rest of creation exists. And it was also only for our sake and for our salvation that the Son of God came down from Heaven and took on our flesh from Mary to redeem us from sin and to give us a share in the glory of His Resurrection from the dead.

Certainly, in view of the infinite expansion of space and time, we feel lost with our average life expectancy of seventy years. And we would have to be self-referentially ashamed of our arrogance if we thought that all the happiness in the world depended on us. However, if we look at the plan of God, whose will it is that all people should be blessed and come to know the truth through Christ, the one Mediator between God and man (see 1 Tim. 2:4-5), then we shall understand the miracle of our existence out of the love that is God Himself (see 1 John 4:8, 16). "The good of the universe is greater than the particular good of one, if we consider both in the same genus. But the good of grace in one is greater than the good of nature in the whole universe."[37] This also means that we can give up our bodily life for others, but we must never

---

[36] Augustine, *Confessions* I, 1, Christian Classics Ethereal Library, http://www.ccel.org/ccel/augustine/confess.html.

[37] Thomas Aquinas, *Summa theologiae* I-II, q. 113, a. 9, ad 2.

break with God. For it is only in the order of grace that the ultimate purpose for which creation exists is revealed to us — namely, in order to be justified by grace.

Our being made in the image and likeness of God, manifested in the act of creation, is deepened at the climax of salvation history into our being in the image and likeness of Christ. For in the Logos, we were chosen, created, and predestined toward His historical presence in the flesh of Jesus Christ.

For as the new Adam, "the man of heaven" (1 Cor. 15:48), Christ is the measure and the image after which we are fashioned, dying with Him and being raised from the dead in Him: *Filius Dei qua homo – imago est hominis* (see 1 Cor. 15:48-49; Rom. 8:29; Rev. 22:13). We only recognize him in the light of faith when we receive Him freely and with total surrender into the dwelling place of our hearts. Only in the willful blindness of the heart can it happen that God comes into His own and His own refuse to receive the Son of God (see John 1:11). It may well be that they deliberately ignore His knocking at the door of their hearts and do not hear His voice, thus depriving themselves of the grace of His entering in and sharing a meal with them (see Rev. 3:20) at the "marriage supper of the Lamb" (Rev. 19:9), to which everyone was invited.

"In their case the god of this world has blinded the minds of the unbelievers, to keep them from seeing the light of the gospel of the glory of Christ, who is the image of God" (2 Cor. 4:4).

But when we open the door to Christ and He shares a meal with us and we with Him, then the light of divine faith is transformed into the vision of God face-to-face; then the eternal light of His glory shines upon us. "And all of us, with unveiled faces, seeing the glory of the Lord as though reflected in a mirror, are being transformed into the same image from one degree of glory to another; for this comes from the Lord, the Spirit" (2 Cor. 3:18).

God's Presence in the Eucharist and in the World

Where man's creatureliness—and, with it, his personal immediacy to God his Creator—is both theoretically and practically denied in favor of the materialistic theory of man as a mere accidental product of a nature playing senselessly with itself, it becomes difficult to make the concept of man's essential nature (*Wesens-Natur*) plausible. At the beginning of the twenty-first century, what we are faced with is basically the alternative of a nihilistic depersonalization of the individual or the assertion of his dignity as a person, which also embraces the corporeal, social, and historical conditions of his existence. Human beings are conceived as living entities by a man and a woman and born of their mother, not artificially manufactured as a product in a scientific or social laboratory. The concept of nature comes from *nasci*, meaning "to be born," and differs from a conglomerate, as the latter cannot have an original subsistence in a living being. In the case of man, it is personhood that unites the human body and soul into an inner unity. *Omne ens est unum.* Man is a creature of God and thus sacred. A technical product, by contrast, is assembled by a created mind, and no human being can breathe the life of the spirit into it.

Karl Marx (1818–1883) wanted to radically emancipate himself from the question of the extraworldly cause of man's completely sensorial-worldly existence. He made use of biblical language but only in order to turn its meaning into the opposite.

> A *being* [*Wesen*] only considers himself independent when he stands on his own feet; and he only stands on his own feet when he owes his existence [*Dasein*] to himself. A man who lives by the grace of another regards himself as a dependent being. But I live completely by the grace of another if I owe him not only the maintenance of my life, but if he has, moreover, *created my life*—if he is the *source* [*Quell*] of my life.

When it is not of my own creation, my life has necessarily a source [*Grund*] of this kind outside of it.[38]

Don't we in the twenty-first century now have the greatest chance of turning our science fictions into reality in a virtual future? Should we, with Richard Dawkins, the doyen of the neo-atheist corps, completely ban religions, "which are to blame for everything"? He is, after all, certain that in the mid-twenty-first century, the successors of Darwin, Watson, and Crick "will destroy the mystical absurdity of souls being detached from bodies." At the double, quick march! "Fifty years on: killing the soul?" But it is only the "soul of the mystics and theologians" that will come in for it, while science will "launch the soul of neuroscientists, computer scientists and science-savvy philosophers to undreamed-of heights."[39] Are we not finally, after biological evolution and the digital revolution, capable of using high-tech programs to create "the best of all possible worlds"[40] in place of the failed God whose creation has turned out to be "the worst of all possible worlds"?[41]

---

[38] Karl Marx, *Nationalökonomie und Philosophie* (1844): id., *Die Frühschriften*, ed. S. Landshut (Stuttgart: Alfred Kröner, 1964), 246. English: *Economic and Philosophic Manuscripts of 1844*, trans. Martin Milligan (2009), third manuscript, no. 5, 48, Marxists Internet Archive, https://www.marxists.org/archive/marx/works/download/pdf/Economic-Philosophic-Manuscripts-1844.pdf.

[39] Richard Dawkins, *Forscher aus Leidenschaft. Gedanken eines Vernunftmenschen* (Berlin: Ullstein, 2018), 237. English: *Science in the Soul: Selected Writings of a Passionate Rationalist* (2017).

[40] Gottfried Wilhelm Leibniz, *Theodizee* I, 8: PhB 71 (Hamburg, 1968), 101.

[41] Arthur Schopenhauer, *Die Welt als Wille und Vorstellung* IV, 46: *Werke in zehn Bänden* IV (Zürich: Diogenes, 1977), 683; cf. Volker Spierling, ed., *Schopenhauer im Denken der Gegenwart* (Munich: Piper, 1987).

God's Presence in the Eucharist and in the World

After many wasted opportunities, has not the time now come to build a "paradise on earth" in a cosmically unbounded living space? Haven't we already reached the point of transcending ourselves out of our real uni-verse and into the "virtual meta-verse of digital immortality"[42] with the help of artificial intelligence, which works perfectly well even without God (and without love)?

Is the homo-deus[43] taking the place of the Deus-Creator and transforming classical humanism into postmodern transhumanism, for which the body is merely biomaterial for the technological will to power with total control over being?[44] Will I become immortal if my brain performance is scanned and my DNA stored as data on a USB stick and at some time downloaded again and enriched with biomass?

Is bisexuality just a crude preliminary stage of the natural sexuality of man and woman that dissolves into a transgenderism where the body is merely the biomaterial waiting to be transformed as its owner chooses, like a slave waiting for the master's command?

In the light of our faith in God's will for our person in its spiritual-bodily nature and in its reflecting in the difference between man and woman the fact that we are created in the image of God, we stand up to anthropological nihilism, asserting the positivity of being and testifying that God is the hope of every human being in his or her life and death.

---

[42] Neal Stephenson, *Snow Crash* (New York: Bantam, 1992).

[43] Yuval Noah Harari, *Homo Deus: A Brief History of Tomorrow* (London: Harvill Secker, 2016).

[44] José Granados, *Theología de la creación. De carne a gloria* (Madrid: Didaskalos, 2020); Alberto Frigerio, *Corpo e Lógos nel Processo identitario. Il caso serio del transgenderismo: bioetica alla prova* (Rome: Cantagalli, 2019).

If any individuals suffer from inferiority complexes, cannot get over being slighted by other people, are tired of life and lack drive, or doubt whether their Creator predestines them for their own sake to "be conformed to the image of his Son" (Rom. 8:29), let all such people lift up their hearts to God, their Father, to Christ, their brother, and to the Holy Spirit, their divine friend, and pray every day at dawn:

> O LORD, our Sovereign,
>> how majestic is your name in all the earth!
>
> You have set your glory above the heavens....
> When I look at your heavens, the work of your fingers,
>> the moon and the stars that you have established;
> what are human beings that you are mindful of them,
>> mortals that you care for them?
>
> Yet you have made them a little lower than God,
>> and crowned them with glory and honour.
> You have given them dominion over the works of
>> your hands;
>> you have put all things under their feet....
> O LORD, our Sovereign,
>> how majestic is your name in all the earth! (Ps. 8:1–9)

Chapter 5

I am the LORD your God
Exodus 20:2

It is not just since Feuerbach's projection theory that there has been a suspicion that people shape and create their gods according to their own image and likeness. Their imagination is said to be the creative energy and their fear the driving force behind the birth of the highly diverse and contradictory images that the various cultures have created of the absolute, of transcendence, of the sacred, of the gods, and of the afterlife. The notion of the gods as persons according to the human model is just one variant of these intellectual creations. And so Israel, too, produced its national god called Yahweh in accordance with its own ideas and needs. Biblical monotheism was, the argument then goes, nothing other than the outcome of a process of the progressive monopolization of the national God. The God of Israel was no more than the genius of the culture of one Near Eastern Semitic tribe and hence one at which an enlightened Central European could only turn up his nose.

Believing that biblical monotheism was itself merely the culturally superior conception of the divine, Gotthold Ephraim Lessing (1729–1781) gave expression in his "Ring Parable" to the enlightened standard model of tolerant religious pluralism. Truth might well exist, but it cannot be expressed in just one religion or philosophy—at most, in all of them together. In each of the three monotheistic religions, the belief in the one God is, so Lessing reflected, complementarily beyond all dogmatic formulae and exclusive cultic rites. "Not the truth which someone possesses or believes he possesses, but the honest effort he has made to get at the truth, constitutes a human being's worth.... If God held fast in his right hand the whole of truth and in his left hand only the ever-active quest for truth, albeit with the proviso that I should constantly and eternally err, and said to me: 'Choose!', I would humbly fall upon his left hand and say: 'Father, give! For pure truth is for you alone!' "[45]

Recently, the Catholic mayor of Palermo confessed to me that he firmly believed in God but did not know His name. This, he said, was because thousands of Islamic immigrants live in his city, so that the homogeneous Christian culture is disintegrating. The common anonymous God, whose truth is reflected in the different names given to Him by the religions, is the paradigm of the political elite in pluralistic societies. In this way, they want to defuse the dogmatic differences between the religions while holding the pluralistic society together with a civil-religious bond.

If we compare all mythical religions and all philosophical approaches to transcendence with the unique faith of the Bible, we can recognize a serious difference. Everywhere we find a spiritual yearning, an ethical striving, and an intellectual plumbing of the divine and the sacred; but the divine and the sacred conceals itself from us or turns into a riddle for ever and, even in its majestic

---

[45] Gotthold Ephraim Lessing, *Eine Duplik* (1778), in *Lessing's Werke* III (Frankfurt a. M.: Insel Verlag, 1967), 321–322. English: *Philosophical and Theological Writings* (Cambridge, UK: Cambridge University Press, 2005), 96.

grandeur, manifests its indifference toward mortals. The primal experience of Israel, on the other hand, is not the finding of a God whom they sought and in whom its own national genius is represented; rather, it is the miracle of being found by Him who sought and visited His people. It is not the people looking for their God, but God looking for His people and setting up His tent among them.

The unique and incomparable feature of the biblical belief in God is, after all, that it is not a case of some people or other choosing or creating its God but rather that Yahweh chooses and creates a people for Himself. Just as "in the beginning" He created (*bara*) the heavens and the earth from His word, so "in the beginning" of salvation history He created (*bara*) a people out of the twelve tribes of Israel. God it was "who created you, O Jacob ... who formed you, O Israel" (Isa. 43:1; cf. 43:7); He promises the people He took possession of as His own: "You shall be holy to me" (Lev. 20:26). "These are the words that you shall speak to the Israelites," God says to Moses at the making of the covenant: "Now therefore, if you obey my voice and keep my covenant, you shall be my treasured possession out of all the peoples. Indeed, the whole earth is mine, but you shall be for me a priestly kingdom and a holy nation" (Exod. 19:5-6). Hence it holds that:

1. God is the subject of creation and of salvation history.
2. God's creative and elective action is the predicate.
3. The covenant people—namely, the Israel of Yahweh and then the Church of Jesus Christ—is the object and fruit of the saving action of the triune God.

What name could man give God? Adam was only commissioned by God to give names to the created entities (cf. Gen. 2:19). But God cannot be named with any name by us. Only He can reveal Himself. Moses, the future mediator of the covenant, does not of Himself know how to answer the Israelites' question in their Egyptian captivity as to what the God of their ancestors is called. But God instructs Moses to say to the Israelites: "I AM has sent me to you" (Exod. 3:14). God is infinite present to Himself in pure being, which is not sundered by the separateness of time and space and constantly needing to put itself back together. He reveals His subsisting self being (*Selbstsein*) as his name for ever, the name by which we call upon Him from one generation to the next. The name of God is:

I AM WHO I AM. (Exod. 3:14)

The term *God* is therefore not the designation for a metaphysical idea or an ethical postulate or the molecular formula of a world theory or the beguiling acoustic pattern of lyrical theopoetics but rather the Person who reveals Himself to me, who instills unconditional trust in me, on whom I can rely completely, and who makes it very easy for me to decide in His favor. "To believe that God—at least *this* God—exists is to believe that you as a person now stand in the presence of God as a Person. What would, a moment before, have been variations in opinion, now become variations in your personal attitude to a Person. You are no longer faced with an argument which demands your assent, but with a Person who demands your confidence."[46]

This is not a definition that circumscribes an individual being (*Seiendes*) through the specific difference within the context of a general classification. The term *God* that we use in our human languages does not denote a mode of appearance, a genus, or the

---

[46] C. S. Lewis, "The World's Last Night," in *The World's Last Night and Other Essays* (New York, 1960), VII 2, https://www.fadedpage. com/books/20210322/html.php#ch7.

general nature (*allgemeines Wesen*) that is realized fictively through many individuals, as is the case in mythological polytheism or pantheism or when we say that there are actually existing individuals who all share the nature of being human. Thus, we say: Socrates is a human being. We are thinking of him in his unrepeatable particularity as a person, the "first substance." But the essence of personhood (i.e., the second substance) can also be expressed (i.e., subsist) through an infinite number of other persons. God's self-revelation in His name "I am who I am" means that the divine nature is identical with His being a person (*Person-Sein*). The "I" of Yahweh is His Being and the "I"-ness (*Ich-Sein*) is His name, by which we call upon Him and by which He addresses His *Word* to us, so that we understand Him in His *Spirit*. The term *God* in the language of the Bible and of the Church's faith and prayer is to be understood personally and relationally. In theological terminology we say, ὁ θεός / *Deus est personaliter sumptum and not essentialiter sumptum.* We always mean the personal God who enacts His essence relationally in Himself and in His inner-divine relations relates Himself to creation and the covenant, thus communicating Himself to mankind as grace and truth.

In the light of the revelation of the Trinity, we say that the immanent processions of the Son from the Father and of the Spirit from the Father and the Son carry on into the world in salvation history in the missions of the Son and of the Spirit. God addresses us personally in His *Word.* And we are permitted—taught by Jesus, the Word made flesh, and sharing in the Son's relation to the Father—to address God in the Holy Spirit as *Abba, Father* (see Rom. 8:15; Gal. 4:6) or, as the Church of the triune God: *Our Father* (see Matt. 6:9).

Jesus does not have a relationship with an abstract Godhead whom He then pictures to Himself as a person by addressing Him in a familiar way as "my Father." In the Old and New Testaments ὁ θεός is always the first person of the Trinity. Through the incarnate Son of the eternal Father, we are really included in the real relations of the triune God as a result of being sons and daughters of God. The fact that Jesus is truly the Son of the Father and our Redeemer from alienation from God is the reason for the truth that we believe — namely, that we are "called children of God; and that is what we are" (1 John 3:1).

In the beginning of the covenant history of God's Chosen People, God reveals His name, which is: I am who I am. When the "time is fulfilled, and the kingdom of God has come near" (Mark 1:15), it is really present in the person of the God-Man, Jesus Christ. He is the autobasileia.[47] Here and now, the Word, who was with God from all eternity and who is God, reveals through the mouth of Jesus the innermost mystery of God, for "there is salvation in no one else, for there is no other *name* under heaven given among mortals by which we must be saved" (Acts 4:12). Our being children and friends of God is real because we have been baptised "*in the name of the Father and of the Son and of the Holy Spirit*" (Matt. 28:19). Then the promise applies to all His disciples: "And remember, I am with you always, to the end of the age" (Matt. 28:20). The name of the "I am who I am" is the "name of the Father and of the Son and of the Holy Spirit." The *name* of God is for not just a liturgical formula or a projection of the inadequate notions and conceptualizations of finite reason onto the unknown mystery beyond its reach. The name "Father and Son and Holy Spirit" is God Himself in the reality of His eternal being and life, who communicated Himself really in Jesus Christ. The mystery of the Trinity is the revelation of the one God in three Persons

[47] Origen, *Comment. in Matthew* 4, 17.

in the identity of His reality and presence, in the unity of God's eternal being (immanent Trinity) and His historical action for our salvation (economic Trinity), of Christology and soteriology.

So God is not definable through the finite and the created. However, the other way around, the world is defined in relation to Him as the creature of Him who does not possess His eternal being through participation but who fulfills it infinitely through His essence (*Wesen*) and is in full possession of Himself. For this reason, God remains an inaccessible mystery for us and yet at the same time draws unsurpassably close to us: "For 'In him we live and move and have our being'" (Acts 17:28).

It is the wrong approach to invoke the dialectical opposition of Greek and biblical thinking in the biblical self-revelation of God in His name "I am who I am" or, like the Reformers, to propound an extreme interpretation of Original Sin as the total loss of any relationship with God. For man's rational nature is a participation in divine reason and therefore ordered toward the knowledge of God. Faith as an act and in its content is an act of total surrender to God with all one's understanding and will, an *obsequium rationabile* (see Rom. 12:2). Faith enlightened by the Holy Spirit is quite the opposite of an irrational sense of total dependence on a suprapersonal Absolute or on an opaque beyond (in the manner of the black holes in the universe), the opposite of an arbitrary option, such as when people say: "There must be something higher." On the Areopagus of Philo-Sophia, the love of wisdom, Christ's Apostle preached the wisdom of love. Everyone should "search for God and perhaps grope for him and find him—though indeed he is not far from each one of us" (Acts 17:27). The faith infused from above as the act and habitus of the supernatural knowledge of God does not mean that the light of reason is switched off but rather that it shines with supreme radiance through the light that "in the beginning" was poured out upon all creation and that came into the world in Christ, the Word of God, as the person of the God-Man.

Thus, it was God Himself, whose eternal power and divinity can be known through the thinking and judgment of reason (see Wisd. 13:1–9; Sir. 17:6–11; Rom. 1:19–20) and who justifies us through our belief in Christ (see Rom 3:22), who personally laid the foundation for the synthesis of reason and faith. In a massive 1,800-page work on the history of ideas from Moses and Plato to analytical philosophy, Jürgen Habermas (b. 1929), a brilliant representative of the Frankfurt School, shows that the "relationship between faith and knowledge" constitutes the true constellation of Western culture.[48] All religions, philosophies, and civilizations move between the two categorial poles of human self-understanding and understanding of the world in the universal, i.e., catholic, view of the transcendental reference of every rational being to God as the origin, meaning, and goal of all creation.

To be sure, the fundamentally human quest for truth and justice is also to be found in God's covenant people. But, given that God makes Himself present, that for which the spiritual nature shared by all human beings strives is achieved through God's grace in the worship of God and obedience to His commandments, which lead us on the path of good. "For what other great nation has a god so near to it as the LORD our God is whenever we call to him?" (Deut. 4:7).

God's nearness to His people, whom He leads out of slavery into the Promised Land and allows to attain redemption through

---

[48] Jürgen Habermas, *Auch eine Geschichte der Philosophie I. Die okzidentale Konstellation von Glauben und Wissen* (Berlin, 2019). English: *This Too a History of Philosophy.*

suffering, is historically realized in an unsurpassable manner in the Incarnation of His Son, Jesus Christ. Jesus proclaimed the nearness and active presence of the Kingdom of God and established the eternal covenant with the New People of God in His blood. And the Lord, who rose from the dead, promises the apostolic community of disciples that He will remain with His Church until the end of time. Thus, the Church as the Body of Christ, of which we are members through Baptism, is not only the instrument of His universal salvific will but also has Christ as her Head and acting subject. *Christus praesens* is the Head of the Body, which, through her members, continues, actualizes, and universalizes the saving work of Christ in the world.

The God who reveals His "I" as eternal Being, which is His essence as immanent self-communication in His Word and Spirit in salvation history, is identical with His presence in the world and in the heart of man. God is the Lord. His divinity does not rule over us as a passive omnipresence of the eternal but is God's active intervention in our favor. For God is God as the Lord—*Dominus Deus Israel.*

He is the King of His Kingdom, the *basileia tou Theou*, which has taken possession of this world in the person of Christ and in His story right up to the Cross and Resurrection. This is why the apostle Thomas could fall down before the Victor over sin and death, acclaiming the God-Man, Jesus Christ, as "My Lord and my God" (John 20:28).

When faced with the contingency of worldly existence and the threat to our eternal and temporal salvation through the wickedness and sin of the world, we do not beat a fearful retreat. For God revealed to His people on their perilous pilgrimage of faith the certainty that "the LORD your God, who is present with you, is a great and awesome God" (Deut. 7:21).

God's Presence in the Eucharist and in the World

Christ is the incarnate Lordship of God. In the Word, who is Himself God, the triune God dwells among us "and we have seen his glory, the glory as of a father's only son, full of grace and truth" (John 1:14). "Jesus is Lord—*Dominus Jesus*" (Rom. 10:9; 1 Cor. 12:3). This is the Church's most primitive confession of the deity of Christ because in *Him* the reign of God is fully realized in history. This is the Church's whole profession of Christ and contains all the truth that was later to be developed in future Christology.

The Kingdom of God came to us as it was historically present in the Incarnation of the Word and in its proclamation in Jesus. It continues to be realized eschatologically in the future when we pray to our Father in Heaven: "Thy will be done, on earth as it is in heaven" (Matt. 6:10, RSVCE). And this brings us to the root of a Christian morality, which goes far beyond the ethics of the natural moral law that is evident to every reasonable person in his or her conscience.

The ethics of Israel are already theocentrically orientated toward a God of personal closeness and not toward a God as guarantor and controller of the principles of natural moral law.

The Decalogue (*deca-logos*) is God's word to us. The Torah stands within the horizon of God's self-revelation: "I am the LORD your God, who brought you out of the land of Egypt, out of the house of slavery" (Exod. 20:2). In the light of the Christ event, this is rightly related to the global redemption from the slavery of ungodliness of the sinner who had turned from a friend into an enemy of God and thus into a slave of sin.

In Jesus, however, a deepening alignment takes place of our will to God's will, so that we become God's friends. "For if while we were enemies, we were reconciled to God through the death of his Son, much more surely, having been reconciled, will we be saved by his life" (Rom. 5:10). Christian ethics lie in following Christ and in the baptized, the members of His Body, being conformed to Christ, their Head. Before His Passion, Jesus prayed in the Garden of Gethsemane: "Father, if you are willing, remove this cup from me; yet, not my will but yours be done" (Luke 22:42). By virtue of the hypostatic union, the human will of Jesus submits historically and concretely to His divine will, which is already essentially one with the eternal will of the Father and the Holy Spirit. In this, Jesus is *sacramentum et exemplum* of the union of our wills with God's salvific will for a life in the Spirit of Christ. Christian, monastic, and priestly mysticism, asceticism, and ethics are incarnationally, sacramentally, and ecclesially grounded. Following Jesus as His disciples means surrendering our wills and sacrificing our lives in "spirit and soul and body" (1 Thess. 5:23) as we tread the path of our life on earth. "And the life I now live in the flesh I live by faith in the Son of God, who loved me and gave himself for me" (Gal. 2:20). Our life "in word or deed" (Col. 3:17) and in our actions and suffering is the glorification of God both with our innate and acquired talents and with the sacramental and charismatic graces given to us by the Holy Spirit. In this way, we serve the ministry of "building up the body of Christ" (Eph. 4:12). "He is the head of the body, the church" (Col. 1:18).

Through the Incarnation, the Son of God became our Redeemer from sins and the founder of our being sons and daughters of God. Thus "he is the mediator of a new covenant" (Heb. 9:15), "a priest for ever, according to the order of Melchizedek" (Heb. 7:17). With His body given as a sacrifice and "with his own blood" he "entered once for all into the Holy Place ... thus obtaining eternal redemption" (Heb. 9:12). Through His sacrifice on the Cross we are sanctified, for "he has perfected for all time those who are sanctified" (Heb. 10:14). We do not need to offer outward sacrifices to God, as the pagans do to their false gods; nor do we have to seek to earn God's good will through great achievements. We give ourselves to God as a gift and sacrifice in conformity with Christ. When He entered the world at His Incarnation, the Son said to the Father: "Sacrifices and offerings you have not desired, but a body you have prepared for me.... See, God, I have come to do your will" (Heb. 10:5, 7). And this we know as the adopted children of God in Christ, who is one God with the Father and the Holy Spirit: "And it is by God's will that we have been sanctified through the offering of the body of Jesus Christ once for all" (Heb. 10:10). This surrender of the body in unity with the will of Christ preserves Christian dogmatics from an ideologization of faith, the liturgy from a hollow ritualism, and morality from a rigorism that is unable to repudiate its twin brother, laxism.

And the liturgical and doxological worship of God in the spirit of Christ that the Apostle urges us to offer is "by the mercies of God, to present your bodies as a living sacrifice, holy and acceptable to God" (Rom. 12:1).

Chapter 6

I am the bread of life

John 6:35

The "I AM" statements of Jesus identify Him as the Revealer of the Father. He is the Son of God, coessential with the Father. He is the Word made flesh. By means of His humanity, He assures mankind of the unsurpassable presence of His divinity. Just as the Father is in the Son and the Son is in the Father as the one God (cf. John 10:30; 14:11), so his disciples dwell in the house of the Father, who has a dwelling-place prepared for everyone (cf. John 14:2). God's house and dwelling place are not the abode of beautiful souls in the realm of ideals, but are the *Christus praesens*, the Church that Christ, the Son of the living God, intended to build on the Rock, on Peter (see Matt. 16:16–18), "the church of the living God, the pillar and bulwark of the truth" (1 Tim. 3:15).

The Father and the Son come to those who believe and love Them, and They make Their home with them (see John 14:23). "On that day you will know that I am in my Father, and you in me, and I in you. They who have my commandments and keep them are those who love me; and those who love me will be loved by my Father, and I will love them and reveal myself to them" (John 14:20-21). Revelation in the Christian sense cannot be reduced to information about truths that surpass natural understanding. Revelation is God's self-communication in grace and truth.

God's Presence in the Eucharist and in the World

In the many human words of Jesus, which Simon Peter, representing the whole Church, recognizes as "the words of eternal life" (John 6:68), the one Divine Word is spoken that in the eternal beginning (without any temporal beginning) was with God and is God. The humanity of Jesus is the "way" by which we reach His divinity, in which Jesus, the Lord, is "the truth and the life" (John 14:6). Human nature serves the divinity of Jesus Christ as the instrument that is personally joined to Him and as the medium through which His divine glory is revealed. Christ's humanity is the primordial sacrament of the communication of reconciliation and of the grace of being a child of God. In the sacrament of the Body and Blood, the flesh of the incarnate Son of God remains forever present in the assembly of His disciples, which, as a visible corporation, is His visible bodily presence as the Church.

Here we have the threefold way of speaking of the Body of Christ, His bodily presence: His historical body in His earthly and transfigured existence, His sacramental Body in the Eucharist, and His ecclesial Body, i.e., His presence in the assembly of His believers.

If their first encounter with the Incarnation of the Divine Word and the death of the Son of God on the Cross—along with His bodily Resurrection—provoked intellectual opposition and a sense of sacred-aesthetic revulsion among the well-educated members of the Greco-Roman culture and its variant in mythological folk religiosity, then it was even more inevitable that the belief that His Flesh and Blood are food and drink for eternal life would arouse indignation at such "religious fanaticism," which apparently went as far as eating human flesh (cannibalism, so-called Thyestean Feasts).

For the bodily presence of the Son of God in the Sacrament of the Altar apparently seemed to them to be merely the ultimate consequence of the mistake made at the start of the duplicity. In the second century, the philosopher Celsus, to whom the Christian scholar Origen (AD 185-253) dedicated an elaborate reply, had formulated the basic principle that seemed to overturn completely the whole Christian mystery: "O Jews and Christians, no God or son of a God either came or will come down (to earth)."[49]

But we Christians believe that God's wisdom is greater and His love more powerful than we can conceive. I trust the Word of God more than my own eyes and the gyrations of my thoughts. What seems impossible to men is possible to God (see Luke 1:37). God is love, and He cares for His creatures like a loving father for His children.

In his great discourse on the Bread from Heaven in the synagogue at Capernaum (see John 6:22-59), Jesus reveals Himself as the bread that God offers and that gives life to the world.

These words of revelation open to us the mystery of the Person and mission of the Word made flesh, the *Verbum Incarnatum*. The full depth of the Incarnation of the Word is revealed in the mystery of the Eucharist. Some exegetes doubt whether the evangelist is intentionally insinuating a reference to the Eucharist. But in the light of the liturgical practice of the early Church, which on the Lord's Day gathered in remembrance of the Cross and Resurrection of her "Lord and God" (John 20:28) for the "breaking of bread" (1 Cor. 10:16; Acts 2:42; 20:11) and the "Lord's supper" (1 Cor. 11:20) at the "Lord's table" (1 Cor. 10:21) and at the "one altar" (see 1 Cor. 10:18; Heb. 13:10) of the Church, there can be no doubt about the sacramental interpretation of the words of the Son of God when He says: "Those who eat my flesh and drink my blood have eternal life, and I will raise them up on the last day; for my flesh is true food and my blood is true drink" (John 6:54-55).

---

[49] Origen, *Contra Celsum* 5, 2.

God's Presence in the Eucharist and in the World

These revelatory words of Jesus, which are so significant for Christology and the doctrine of the Eucharist, were preceded as signs by the healing of the sick and the multiplication of the loaves and fish for the hungry crowd. The miracle of the loaves, which served to satisfy physical hunger and to sustain physical life, is introduced with words that recall the institution of the Eucharist at the Last Supper: "Then Jesus *took* the loaves, and when he had *given thanks* [*eucharistesas*] he *distributed* them to those who were seated (John 6:11). This sign identifies Jesus in the eyes of the faithful Jews as "the prophet who is to come into the world" (John 6:14) according to God's promise. In contrast to false prophets, pagan oracles, necromancers, and sorcerers, who are an abomination to the Lord, this refers to the new prophet according to Moses, of whom the God of the covenant with His Chosen People said: "I will raise up for them a prophet like you from among their own people; I will put my words in the mouth of the prophet, who shall speak to them everything that I command" (Deut. 18:18).

Jesus, who, as an empathetic teacher, knows the priorities of the people, directs the eyes of those who seek divine signs to God's truth, which infinitely transcends all earthly expectations and needs. Earthly pleasures and perishable food cannot satisfy and make blessed those who "hunger and thirst for righteousness" (Matt. 5:6). And this is why Jesus admonishes everyone who wants to become His disciple: "Do not work for the food that perishes, but for the food that endures for eternal life, which the Son of Man will give you. For it is on him that God the Father has set his seal" (John 6:27).

And everyone who believes in Jesus, who was sent by the Father, is therefore acting in accordance with God's wishes. The bread that the Israelites once miraculously received in the life-threatening wilderness had been sent down to them from Heaven, not by Moses, but by Jesus' Father. "For the bread of God is that which comes down from heaven and gives life to the world" (John 6:33). Jesus' listeners now think that this bread is some kind of long-lasting food whose nutrients are never depleted by being digested, and they are quite enraptured by the thought of being freed from the burden of procuring their daily food: "Sir, give us this bread always" (John 6:34). But Jesus is not a purveyor of some highly convenient magic potion. He is the visible presence of God, who welcomes us through faith and love into His eternal life and forcibly frees us from the golden cage of superficial needs and entertainment programs that cater to the slogan *panem et circenses*. Jesus is in His person the fulfillment of the longing for the life of God in us. That is why He, the Word of God made flesh, answers the people of His covenant:

> I am the bread of life. Whoever comes to me will never be hungry, and whoever believes in me will never be thirsty … for I have come down from heaven, not to do my own will, but the will of him who sent me. And this is the will of him who sent me, that I should lose nothing of all that he has given me, but raise it up on the last day. This is indeed the will of my Father, that all who see the Son and believe in him may have eternal life; and I will raise them up on the last day. (John 6:35, 38–40)

When, following this self-revelation of the Son of God, the evangelist addresses the topic of Jesus' claim to having, contrary to the "murmuring of the Jews," an exclusive soteriological meaning for our ultimate relationship with God, this naturally does not refer anachronistically to the "Jewish faith community," as later contrasted to the "Christian community of salvation." Rather, it refers to the biblical People of God who are to recognize God in the humanity of Christ and confess Him in faith.

How can this fellow villager, playmate, and local lad named Jesus, Son of Joseph, whose father and mother we know well, speak of Himself in a grotesque contradiction to His humble origins as "bread from heaven" and as food for eternal life?

But at this critical moment, Jesus reveals His true origin from God, His Father. His relationship to him is the "relationship of the Son" according to both His divinity and the humanity He assumed from the Virgin Mary. This is what the Christological dogma says in accordance with the overall biblical testimony—namely, that there are not two Sons of God, as is postulated by the heresy of Adoptianism, which does not permit the relationship of the man Jesus to God to subsist in the relationship of the eternal Word to the Father. There is no dual original relationship to God of Jesus as God or as man; otherwise, Jesus would only be adoptively linked to God according to His humanity and not hypostatically. For human nature subsists in the eternal relation of the Son to the Father. Even to us, the disciples of Jesus who daily fight our way forward through a desert of temptations and doubts along the path of discipleship toward faith in Jesus, the following words are addressed by Jesus:

> Do not complain among yourselves. No one can come to me unless drawn by the Father who sent me; and I will raise that person up on the last day. It is written in the prophets, 'And they shall all be taught by God.' Everyone who has heard and learned from the Father comes to me. Not that anyone has seen the Father except the one who is from God; he has seen the Father. Very truly, I tell you, whoever believes has eternal life. I am the bread of life. Your ancestors ate the manna in the wilderness, and they

died. This is the bread that comes down from heaven, so that one may eat of it and not die. I am the living bread that came down from heaven. Whoever eats of this bread will live for ever; and the bread that I will give for the life of the world is my flesh. (John 6:43–51)

The flesh of the Son of Man is the flesh of the Word that the Son of the Father assumed and that is marked by the wounds of the scourged and crucified Christ by which we have been healed (see Isa. 53:5). The mystery of the person and mission of Jesus, who gives His flesh for the life of the world, can be understood only in His sacrificial death on the Cross. "For God so loved the world that he gave his only Son, so that everyone who believes in him may not perish but may have eternal life" (John 3:16). Here the inner connection is displayed in the dynamic from the Incarnation of the Divine Word to the redemptive sacrificial offering of Christ on the altar of the Cross to His enduring presence in the eucharistic Sacrament of His Body and Blood.

Only those who reflect on the mystery of God's love in the Holy Spirit are able to get beyond the resistance of the rational mind as well as the positivistic limitation of their horizons; for the flesh of man is useless without the Spirit of God (John 6:63), and man's corruptible "flesh and blood cannot inherit the kingdom of God" (1 Cor. 15:50) by itself without the power of God.

Here we must turn our gaze toward Christ:

The one who is of the earth belongs to the earth and speaks about earthly things. The one who comes from heaven is above all. He testifies to what he has seen and heard.... Whoever has accepted his testimony has certified this, that God is true. He whom God has sent speaks the words of God, for he gives the Spirit without measure. The Father loves the Son and has placed all things in his hands. Whoever believes in the Son has eternal life. (John 3:31–36)

And once again, the mild or fiercely skeptical doubts arise here regarding the Incarnation of the Word and the Word's power to be food for eternal life. How can anyone in his right mind want to give us his flesh to eat and try to persuade us of it with the guarantee of immortality?

Between the extreme misunderstandings of the physical eating of material human flesh and its spiritualistic reduction to an assimilation of attitudes, Jesus Himself points to the salvific realism of it. And this is the basis for the sacramental presence of His Body offered up on the Cross and His Blood, which was poured out, under the species of bread and wine. Under these species, He is sacramentally, really present and yet hidden from view in the whole reality of His divinity and humanity. He is God's being there for the salvation of the world, and He mediates eternal life to us in the communion of Father and Son in the Holy Spirit. Let us put our trust completely in the divine word that is spoken to us out of Jesus' human mouth:

> Very truly, I tell you, unless you eat the flesh of the Son of Man and drink his blood, you have no life in you. Those who eat my flesh and drink my blood have eternal life, and I will raise them up on the last day; for my flesh is true food and my blood is true drink. Those who eat my flesh and drink my blood abide in me, and I in them. Just as the living Father sent me, and I live because of the Father, so whoever eats me will live because of me. This is the bread that came down from heaven, not like that which your ancestors ate, and they died. But the one who eats this bread will live for ever. (John 6:53–58)

I am the bread of life

What does the Church teach about the mystery of the Eucharist?

At the Last Supper, on the night when he was betrayed, our Saviour instituted the eucharistic sacrifice of his Body and Blood. He did this in order to perpetuate the sacrifice of the Cross throughout the centuries until he should come again, and so to entrust to his beloved spouse, the Church, a memorial of his death and resurrection: a sacrament of love, a sign of unity, a bond of charity, a paschal banquet in which Christ is eaten, the mind is filled with grace, and a pledge of future glory is given to us.[50]

---

[50] Second Vatican Council, Constitution on the Sacred Liturgy *Sacrosanctum Concilium* (December 4, 1963), no. 47.

Chapter 7

This is my body
Mark 14:22

In Jesus' great discourse at Capernaum, our knowledge of the real and sacramental, i.e., real-symbolic, presence of the Word of God in the flesh of Christ was, following the approach of Johannine theology, directly derived from the self-revelation of His divinity.

The three Synoptic Gospels lead us to a knowledge of Jesus' divinity from the perspective of His humanity. If we add the Pauline version (see 1 Cor. 11:23–25), we have four accounts of the institution of the Eucharist, the Sacrament of Sacraments, during the Last Supper on the night before His salvation-bringing suffering and death on the Cross. They differ in nuance and agree in substance. Jesus is not just any prophet but the Son, known only to the Father, who wants solely to reveal God, His Father, to mankind (see Matt. 11:27; Luke 10:22). In the clear knowledge of the salvific relevance of His offering Himself to the Father, He accepts the unjust human judgment passed on Him. In this way, He transforms sinners' godlessness and enmity toward God into their reconciliation with God (see 2 Cor. 5:20). For He is the sole Mediator between the one God and the many people (see 1 Tim. 2:5). "The mediator of a new covenant" (Heb. 9:15) "entered once for all into the Holy Place, not with the blood of goats and calves, but with his own blood, thus obtaining eternal redemption" (Heb.

9:12). For "the blood of Christ, who through the eternal Spirit of-fered himself without blemish to God, [will] purify our conscience from dead works to worship the living God!" (Heb. 9:14).

The sacramental celebration of the Cross and Resurrection in the Holy Mass is therefore not a staged reenactment of the Last Supper, a sentimental agape celebration, or a religious ceremony aimed at strengthening the sense of community. Rather, it is the real memorial and objective making present of the sacrificial of-fering in the words of Christ spoken by the priest and in the sacramental signs of bread and wine. Here, however, Christ is not the object of the memorial. We, as members of His Body, are not the primary subject of memorial; rather, Christ is the Head of the Church and the actual giver of all the graces we receive in the seven sacraments of the Church. In all the other sacraments, we speak of an actual presence of Christ, who lives and reigns with the Father as the risen Lord and who always intercedes for us before God as the High Priest of the heavenly and earthly liturgy. But in the Eucharist, He is present not only as the agent, but "truly, really, and substantially," i.e., in the real substance of His human nature, which—hypostatically linked to His divinity—is Christ Himself, the Word of God made flesh.

The eucharistic Real Presence means not only the factual presence of the Body of Jesus in space but also the offering of Himself as food, so that through it we may have communion with the life of God in us. Just as the Son lives in Trinitarian community from the Father and owes His divinity eternally to Him, so we live in community with the Father and the Son in the Holy Spirit through our sacramental and ecclesial incorpora-tion into His incarnationally assumed human body. Sacramental communion realizes our participation in the perichoresis of the Divine Persons in God's being. God's being is essentially eternal communion of love (see 1 John 4:7–9). Jesus, the Word made flesh, the divine Son who rests at the heart of the Father, reveals to us this truth of our communion with the Most Holy Trinity through communion with His incarnate body in his human words when He says:

> Those who eat my flesh and drink my blood have eternal life, and I will raise them up on the last day; for my flesh is true food and my blood is true drink. Those who eat my flesh and drink my blood abide in me, and I in them. Just as the living Father sent me, and I live because of the Father, so whoever eats me will live because of me. This is the bread that came down from heaven, not like that which your ancestors ate, and they died. But the one who eats this bread will live for ever. (John 6:54–58)

Human nature is an abstract term, but it denotes what concretely constitutes the flesh-and-blood human being. Man is not the form-giving principle of his soul, which dwells in a body like a king in his castle or the beggar in his hut. Matter is the principle of our individuation. This means that his or her respective human body is the existence of this concrete human being. The body, therefore, means our concrete, four-dimensional existence in space and time. Blood is an integral part of our corporeality. But it also signifies the difference between the human body and a physical body insofar as it means the body's life both in reality and symbolically. Humans are not lumps of wood but rather are beings of flesh and blood. The blood flows through the heart, which pumps it around the whole human body. Woe betide us if our blood is sick or if the brain is not supplied sufficiently with oxygen and the muscles are not regularly perfused. Our lifeblood, the blood of the heart, denotes our will and a duty to "love the

Lord your God with all your heart, and with all your soul, and with all your mind … [and] your neighbour as yourself" (Matt. 22:37-39).

The faith of the Church clearly states that the whole Christ is fully present with His divinity and humanity in each of the two eucharistic species. The faithful who receive Holy Communion under the species of bread alone are therefore not deprived of the Real Presence of Christ or of receiving sacramental grace. With respect to the presence of Christ in the two separate species of bread and wine, it is legitimate to associate with the Body of Christ first and foremost the revealed truth of His substantial presence and with the Blood of Christ first and foremost the truth of His sacrifice through which the world is freed from Original Sin and men and women are redeemed from their sins.

During or after the Passover meal, in which God's people commemorate the Exodus from the land of bondage, Jesus *took* bread in His hands, *spoke* the great prayer of thanksgiving over it, *broke* it, and *gave* it to his disciples saying: "Take, eat; this is my body" (Mark 14:22; Matt. 26:26). The action of taking, breaking and giving the bread together with the performative words of the divine Lord, who transforms the bread into His body and makes the visible bread a sign of His invisible presence in His crucified and glorified body, is the substance of the Eucharist of the Church.

Paul and Luke add a specifying relative clause that underlines the sacrificial nature of Christ's death on the Cross: "This is my body, which is given for you" (Luke 22:19) and: "This is my body that is (broken) for you" (1 Cor. 11:24).

By taking the bread in His hands, Jesus displays His will to make the bread a real symbol of His life-imparting presence through the divine power of His words. He offers us His Body as food and

His Blood as drink under visible species. With His words and the power of His messianic Spirit, He consecrates bread and wine in such a way that these signs and nourishment of natural life are transformed into the signs and nourishment of supernatural life. Through Communion with Jesus in His Flesh and Blood, we share in His divinity and thus in His community of life with the Father in the Holy Spirit.

Just as the mystery of the Incarnation surpasses the capacity and judgment of the finite mind, it is impossible to make the transubstantiation of bread and wine into the inner reality of Christ's Flesh and Blood plausible to the reasoning of natural thinking by drawing analogies to natural transformation processes in material and ideal nature. The Magisterium has rejected all attempts to weaken the Real Presence in the sense of a spiritualistic symbolization. But the idea of a transformation of the matter into other states of aggregation is also completely erroneous. The human mind can only conceive of the realization of passive possibilities. God's logic, however, in which we participate in the light of faith, says that God has all active possibilities at His disposal. He alone, through his almighty word, can bring into existence that which is not (see Rom. 4:17). Thus, through His almighty word, He transforms the substance of the bread and wine into the substance of the Body and Blood of Christ so that when we ingest them as food and drink, we truly share the Flesh and Blood of Christ. Thus, He becomes food for eternal life when we receive Him into our hearts in faith and love, so that we live from Him as sons and daughters of God. Theology's recourse to Aristotle's category of substance did not serve to reduce the supernatural truth of faith to a natural truth of reason but served instead to distinguish between divine reality and pious fiction or, rather, the dissipation of our relationship to God into a religious worldview.

God's Presence in the Eucharist and in the World

The world, which was created by God, points in all its phenomena symbolically to God, who lives and gives life. In His goodness, He gives us the bread that strengthens the heart. He gives us the wine that gladdens the human heart (see Ps. 104:15). The symbolism of bread and wine, which we encounter already in the sacrifice of Melchisedek (see Gen. 14:19; Ps. 110:4; Heb. 5:6; 7:2, 17), is taken up by Jesus and filled with His incarnational presence. Man cannot encounter God merely as a spiritual abstraction but has need of sensorial-bodily mediation. Our body is the being there of our personal self in the world that God entered through the Incarnation and in which He was always already really present as Creator and Sustainer of our lives. The apostles encountered God by seeing, hearing, and touching Jesus in His bodily existence and thus also entered into a relationship with His Divine Person that was mediated through the senses. The paschal Lord, therefore, also wanted to be sensorially mediated and present as food and drink for eternal life. But He is not visible in His historical, natural mode of existence in four-dimensional corporeality. He makes present the Flesh and Blood of His transfigured human nature, which is seated at the right hand of God in Heaven, under the assumed appearance of bread and wine. His bodily presence with His Flesh and Blood is mediated and represented in the assembly of His disciples through His proclaimed word and through the sacramental forms of bread and wine. But these contain Christ in His Body and Blood, actually and really, *per modum substantiae* [in the manner of substance]. The visible species of bread and wine are the sacramental signs and media (*sacramentum tantum*) of the Real Presence of Christ with his flesh and blood in the consecrated Host and in the consecrated chalice of wine. They are reality and means (*res et sacramentum*) for the salvation of eternal life (*res sacramenti*) — namely, the inner fruitful participation in Christ's humanity and divinity.

Nor does the inner logic of the transubstantiation of bread and wine into the substance of the Body and Blood of Christ depend on the turn toward natural philosophy in recent natural science, which restricts the concept of "substance" to the specific composition of material elements (i.e., meaning only the *causa materialis* of something really existing in the world). Faith rests on the Logos of God, in whom it participates in the Holy Spirit. The eucharistic transubstantiation is founded on the symbolic nature of the created and thus on its capacity to receive God's real communication of Himself as the truth and life of man, who exists concretely in His bodily, social, and historical world. The mystery of the Real Presence of Christ in His transfigured body is rooted in the original miracle of God's Incarnation.

What is the miracle before which we fall to our knees to worship Christ with the words of the apostle Thomas: "My Lord and my God"?

What does the Church believe, based on the words of Christ, about His Real Presence in the liturgy and in the Church?

To accomplish so great a work [salvation in sacrifice and sacrament], Christ is always present in his Church, especially in her liturgical celebrations. He is present in the sacrifice of the Mass, not only in the person of his minister, "the same now offering, through the ministry of priests, who formerly offered himself on the cross" [Council of Trent, Doctrine on the Most Holy Sacrifice of the Mass, chap. 5], but especially under the Eucharistic species. By his power he is present in the sacraments, so that when a man baptizes it is really Christ himself who baptizes. He is present in his Word, since it is he himself who speaks when the Holy Scriptures are read in the Church. He is present, lastly, when the Church prays and sings, for he promised: "Where two or three are gathered together in my name, there am I in the midst of them" (Mt. 18:20).

Christ, indeed, always associates the Church with himself in this great work wherein God is perfectly glorified and men are sanctified. The Church is his beloved Bride who calls to her Lord, and through him offers worship to the Eternal Father.

Rightly, then, the liturgy is considered as an exercise of the priestly office of Jesus Christ. In the liturgy the sanctification of the man is signified by signs perceptible to the senses, and is effected in a way which corresponds with each of these signs; in the liturgy the whole public worship is performed by the Mystical Body of Jesus Christ, that is, by the Head and his members.

From this it follows that every liturgical celebration, because it is an action of Christ the priest and of his Body which is the Church, is a sacred action surpassing all others; no other action of the Church can equal its efficacy by the same title and to the same degree.[51]

---

[51] Second Vatican Council, *Sacrosanctum concilium* 7.

Chapter 8

This is my blood
Mark 14:24

The Church, faithfully following the tradition of the apostles, celebrates the Eucharist, which the Son of God, our Lord, commanded the disciples at the Last Supper to celebrate as a perpetual memorial of His Passion. Through communion with the Son of God in the Body of Christ, we have communion with the triune God and share in His eternal life in the love of the Father and of the Son and of the Holy Spirit. "The cup of blessing that we bless, is it not a sharing in the blood of Christ?" (1 Cor. 10:16). Drinking from this cup of the Blood of Christ that was shed on the Cross grants us communion with the perichoresis of the three Divine Persons.

> Very truly, I tell you, unless you eat the flesh of the Son of Man and drink his blood, you have no life in you. Those who eat my flesh and drink my blood have eternal life, and I will raise them up on the last day.... Those who eat my flesh and drink my blood abide in me, and I in them. Just as the living Father sent me, and I live because of the Father, so whoever eats me will live because of me. (John 6:53–57)

Paul reminds the Corinthians that after the words over the bread, Jesus took the cup and handed it to His disciples, saying: "This cup is the new covenant in my blood" (1 Cor. 11:25). And the Apostle adds by way of explanation: "For as often as you eat this bread and drink the cup, you proclaim the Lord's death until he comes. Whoever, therefore, eats the bread or drinks the cup of the Lord in an unworthy manner will be answerable for the body and blood of the Lord" (1 Cor. 11:26–27).

Paul had already shown that he is clearly aware of the somatic Real Presence, i.e., that he believes Christ to be physically present in His Body and Blood under the species of bread and wine, and teaches it unambiguously when he speaks of the incompatibility of participating at the same time in the Lord's Supper and in pagan or other religious cultic celebrations: "I speak as to sensible people; judge for yourselves what I say. The cup of blessing that we bless [the eucharistic words of consecration], is it not a sharing in the blood of Christ? The bread that we break, is it not a sharing in the body of Christ? Because there is one bread, we who are many are one body, for we all partake of the one bread" (1 Cor. 10:15–17).

In the Consecration of the wine and the offering of communion with His Blood, Jesus anticipated His sacrifice on the Cross both symbolically and really in the Upper Room. The institution of the Blessed Sacrament at the Last Supper is thus the sacramental anticipation of the Sacrifice of the Cross, while the eucharistic Sacrifice of the Holy Mass is the sacramental making present of it. The Church therefore celebrates the Divine Liturgy as the Sunday real memorial of the Paschal Mystery of the Cross and Resurrection of Jesus until He comes again and all the saved are received into the eternal "home of God … among mortals" (Rev. 21:3). For the blood of Christ, which flowed from His wounds in His sacrifice on the altar of the Cross, is the "blood of the (new) covenant which is poured out for many" (Mark 14:24; Luke 22:20), to which is added in Matthew "for the forgiveness of sins" (26:28). Even to the Gentiles, to whom the God of the covenant with Israel was distant and alien, the promise applies: "But now in Christ Jesus you who once were far off have been brought near by the blood of Christ" (Eph. 2:13).

The reference is obvious here to the blood of the covenant that Moses sprinkled on the people when the peace offerings were sacrificed (Exod. 24:8) and to God's New Covenant with His people (see Jer. 31:31; Zech. 9:11) in the blood of His Son. Equally important is the application of the vicarious atoning death of the Servant of God for "the sin of many" (Isa. 53:12). Only in this way can we understand Christ's death on the Cross as a sacrifice of reconciliation. "In Christ God was reconciling the world to himself, not counting their trespasses against them, and entrusting the message of reconciliation to us" (2 Cor. 5:19). Paul and Timothy, the authors of the Second Letter to the Corinthians, then make the link to the priestly-liturgical ministry of the apostles and their successors in the episcopate and priesthood in the post-Easter Church: "So we are ambassadors for Christ, since God is making his appeal through us; we entreat you on behalf of Christ, be reconciled to God" (2 Cor. 5:20). Through the blood of Christ, the Gentiles, too, have come near to God and form the new eschatological community of salvation made up of "Jews and Gentiles." For it was Christ's will to "reconcile both groups to God in one body through the cross ... for through him both of us have access in one Spirit to the Father.... In [Christ] you also are built together spiritually into a dwelling-place for God" (Eph. 2:16, 18, 22).

In view of Christ's self-revelation as handed down to us in the testimony of the early Church, there can be no doubt about the Cross as the sacrifice of the New Covenant, the eucharistic liturgy as the sacramental making present of Christ's historical once-for-all sacrifice on the Cross and the sempiternal heavenly liturgy of Jesus' giving Himself to the Father. The sacrifice of Jesus' offering His life on the Cross is already revealed in advance in the Son's thanksgiving for the gift of divinity received in the eternal procession of the Son from the Father. He gratefully offers His divinity to the Father. And the love of both of them is united eternally and temporally in the Holy Spirit. For "how much more will the blood of Christ, who through the eternal Spirit offered himself without blemish to God, purify our conscience from dead works to worship the living God!" (Heb. 9:14). We share in the Trinitarian communion of love via sacramental Communion with the eucharistic Body and Blood of Christ. In His Incarnation and voluntary self-emptying to death on the Cross (see Phil. 2:6–11), he pinned down and encircled sin as man's refusal to show the necessary gratitude to God for having been created. Therefore, not only was sin forgiven, but guilt was obliterated and completely dissolved in the infinite sea of the Son's ever greater love for the eternal Father. In this way, our Eucharist is a real sharing in Jesus' thanksgiving for the eternal gift of His divinity. What marks its celebration is the offering of His human life for the salvation of the world.

In the sacrifice, we, the members of the Body of Christ, give thanks to God the Father in the Holy Spirit. We give thanks in the Holy Spirit through the Head of the Church, for "I live by faith in the Son of God, who loved me and gave himself for me" (Gal. 2:20) as "a fragrant offering and sacrifice to God" (Eph. 5:2). So we do not stand like outsiders applauding a successful divine performance, the heroic deed of a good person for our benefit. God cannot be worshipped and influenced by outward sacrifices, as with the pagans. The true worship of God consists in the sacrifice of the Church, when we are asked "by the mercies of God, to present your bodies [= our earthly existence] as a living sacrifice, holy and acceptable to God" (Rom. 12:1).

The Sacrifice of the Mass is therefore the sacramental making present of the Sacrifice of the Cross. The Mass is a sacrifice of praise (*hostia laudis*) and thanksgiving (*eu-charistia*). It is worship and glorification of God through and in Christ, who is the Head of the Church. And in the Mass, the sacrifices of supplication and propitiation are effective not on their own account but, rather, on account of the reconciliation brought about by God, which is turned toward us in our daily sins and faults in the measure to which we are spiritually conformed to Christ.[52] We Christians certainly should not sin. "But if anyone does sin, we have an advocate with the Father, Jesus Christ the righteous; and he is the atoning sacrifice for our sins, and not for ours only but also for the sins of the whole world" (1 John 2:1–2).

Original sin is blotted out once and for all in the baptized person who asks for this sacrament in faith, and all of that person's personal sins are forgiven. The baptized are incorporated into the Body of Christ, His human nature. Being a child of God means participating in the personal relationship of the Son to the Father in the Holy Spirit, thanks to Christ's Incarnation and our own sacramental incorporation into the ecclesial Body of Christ. Those who wish to receive Holy Communion and are aware of having committed a grave sin "that is mortal" (1 John 5:16) must first obtain forgiveness through the Sacrament of Reconciliation or at least repent of their sins with perfect contrition and resolve to confess them to a priest at the earliest opportunity.

In the Lutheran Confessio Augustana (CA 24), the Sacrifice of the Mass is completely misunderstood by the Reformers since—based on the assumption that it was a human work of self-justification—they implied that Catholics understood the Sacrifice of the Cross as

---

[52] Council of Trent, Session 21, DH 1753.

merely taking away Original Sin whereas they allegedly accredited the Sacrifice of the Mass with taking away grave post-baptismal sins. Thus, they argued, the wrathful God would be reconciled through the human work of the Sacrifice of the Mass. In reality, however, Catholics believe that the Sacrifice of the Mass is identical in its substance with the Sacrifice of the Cross and differs from it only as a liturgical rite. In the one and the same sacrifice — i.e., on the Cross and when it is made liturgically present — the Son, as Head of the Church and of all creation, offers Himself to God the Father, at the same time including all the members of His Body in His loving self-giving to the Father. Furthermore, God is not reconciled because His "wrath at the sin of the world" would be an immanent alteration of His divine being or even a disturbance of His Trinitarian relationship to Himself but because He corrects and remedies our disturbed relationship to Him, the God of triune love.

The term *opus operatum* for the objective efficacy of the sacraments has nothing to do with the fact that the Holy Mass is a human work with the aim of being justified before God. What is meant by it is rather the efficacy of the sacrament, which does not work through the piety of the minister or the recipient but through Christ Himself, who is the actual minister of grace. The Sacrifice of the Mass does not have an effect with God of itself as a liturgical rite but rather as a sacramental mode of making present the Sacrifice of the Cross. Admittedly, the effect of the Mass — namely, the making present of the Sacrifice of the Cross and the fruits that spring from it for Christians who participate devoutly in the celebration — does not lie in God's reaction to human actions. It is, in fact, the other way around: our giving of our lives to God is an effect of His grace, the grace in which He has reconciled us to Himself. That is the New Covenant in the Blood of Christ.

Luther accuses the Sacrifice of the Mass of supplementing the effect of the Sacrifice of the Cross and turning the instrumental mediation of God's gift to us into a human work or a sacrifice through which we acquire and earn grace. But this argument leads nowhere for the simple reason that we know from the general doctrine of the sacraments that they bring about grace only instrumentally, whereas it is God alone, "*solus Deus*" (!), who produces the inner grace and effect—here, the Real Presence of the Flesh and Blood of Jesus as a representation of His death on the Cross.

Three centuries before Luther's misinterpretation, Thomas Aquinas (1225–1274), the *Doctor Communis*, had already explained the Catholic teaching as follows:

> But that which is the sacramental effect is not impetrated by the prayer of the Church or of the minister, but through the merit of Christ's Passion, the power of which operates in the sacraments.... Wherefore the sacramental effect is made no better by a better minister. And yet something in addition may be impetrated for the receiver of the sacrament through the devotion of the minister: but this is not the work of the minister, but the work of God Who hears the minister's prayer.[53]

The benefit of the many Masses that originate from Christ's command "Do this in remembrance of me" does not lie in any addition to the Sacrifice of the Cross in terms of content but rather in the actual connection of the Christians who are disciples of the crucified and risen Lord. More than eleven hundred years before the emergence of Protestantism, St. Augustine already stated: "This is the sacrifice of Christians: we, being many, are one body in

---

[53] Thomas Aquinas, *Summa theologiae* III, q. 64, a. 1, ad 2.

Christ. And this also is the sacrifice which the Church continually celebrates in the sacrament of the altar, known to the faithful, in which she teaches that she herself is offered in the offering she makes to God."[54]

For those who see in the Catholic Eucharist and the Protestant Lord's Supper merely different ritual versions of an inner-worldly communal experience with a subjective remembrance of Jesus as a great personality from the distant past or view Him as a kind of Mahatma Gandhi and Dalai Lama for the present, the question of the relationship between the Sacrifice of the Cross and the Sacrifice of the Mass must seem like some kind of shadowboxing. If Christ's death on the Cross is valued only as someone's admirable and exemplary faithfulness to His conviction, this constitutes a radical failure to recognize universal significance for salvation. If Jesus had not died for our sins and been raised from the dead, our faith would be "futile," and we would still be in our sins; "then those also who have fallen asleep in Christ have perished" (1 Cor. 15:17–18).

Almost five hundred years after the great controversy over the Sacrifice of the Mass, which is crucial for the truth of the Catholic understanding of Christianity, it is still fitting to take another look at the teaching of the Council of Trent on the Sacrifice of the Mass:

Chapter 1. The Institution of the Most Holy Sacrifice of the Mass

As the apostle testifies, there was no perfection under the former covenant because of the insufficiency of the Levitical priesthood. It was, therefore, necessary (according to the merciful ordination of God the Father) that another priest arise "according to the order of Melchizedek, our

[54] Augustine, *De civitate Die* 10, 6.

Lord Jesus Christ, who could make perfect all who were to be sanctified and bring them to fulfilment (cf. Heb 10:14).

He, then, our Lord and God, was once for all to offer himself to God the Father by his death on the altar of the Cross to accomplish *for them* [there] an everlasting redemption. But, because his priesthood was not to end with his death, at the Last Supper, "on the night when he was betrayed" (1 Cor 11:23),

> in order to leave to his beloved Spouse the Church, a visible sacrifice (as the nature of man demands) — by which the bloody (sacrifice) that he was once for all to accomplish on the Cross would be re-presented, its memory perpetuated until the end of the world, and its salutary power applied for the forgiveness of the sins that we daily commit — declaring himself constituted a priest forever according to the order of Melchizedek (Ps 109:4; Heb 5:6; 7:17),

he offered his body and blood under the species of bread and wine to God the Father, and, under the same signs, gave them to partake of to the disciples (whom he then established as priests of the New Covenant) and ordered them and their successors in the priesthood to offer, saying: "Do this in remembrance of me", etc. (Lk 22:19; 1 Cor 11:24), as the Catholic Church has always understood and taught.

For, after he celebrated the old Pasch, which the multitude of the children of Israel offered to celebrate the memory of the departure from Egypt, Christ instituted a new Pasch, namely, himself, to be offered by the Church through her priests under visible signs in memory of his passage from this world to the Father, when by the shedding of his blood he redeemed us, "delivered us from the dominion of darkness, and transferred us to his kingdom" (Col 1:13).

This is the clean oblation that cannot be defiled by any unworthiness or malice on the part of those who offer it and that the Lord foretold through Malachi would be offered in all places as a clean oblation to his name (Mal 1:11). The apostle Paul also refers clearly to it when, writing to the Corinthians, he says that those who have been defiled by partaking of the table of devils cannot be partakers of the table of the Lord (1 Cor 10:21). By "table" he understands "altar" in both cases. Finally, this is the [oblation] that was prefigured by various types of sacrifices under the regime of nature and of the law. For it includes all the good that was signified by those former sacrifices; it is their fulfilment and perfection.[55]

Chapter 2. The Visible Sacrifice Is Propitiatory for the Living and the Dead

In this divine sacrifice that is celebrated in the Mass, the same Christ who offered himself once in a bloody manner (Heb 9:14, 27f.) on the altar of the Cross is contained and is offered in an unbloody manner. Therefore, the holy council teaches that this sacrifice is truly propitiatory, so that, if we draw near to God with an upright heart and true faith, with fear and reverence, with sorrow and repentance, through it "we may receive mercy and find grace to help in time of need" (Heb 4:16). For the Lord, appeased by this oblation,

[55] DH 1739–1742.

grants grace and the gift of repentance, and he pardons wrongdoings and sins, even great ones. For, the victim is one and the same: the same now offers himself through the ministry of priests who then offered himself on the Cross; only the manner of offering is different.

The fruits of this oblation (the bloody one, that is) are received in abundance through this unbloody oblation. By no means, then, does the latter detract from the former. Therefore, it is rightly offered according to apostolic tradition, not only for the sins, punishments, satisfaction, and other necessities of the faithful who are alive, but also for those who have died in Christ but are not wholly purified.[56]

[56] Ibid., 1743.

Chapter 9

Nor did his flesh see corruption

Acts 2:31

The bodily Resurrection of Christ is the prerequisite of our being raised in our then-no-longer-mortal but immortal "spiritual body" (1 Cor. 15:44). Christ is not metaphorically risen into the existential faith of people who live according to His ideals. His Resurrection is an event in history like the Incarnation, the actual coming of God into this world and His presence in the Body of Christ. "If Christ has not been raised, your faith is futile and you are still in your sins. Then those also who have fallen asleep in Christ have perished" (1 Cor. 15:17–18).

Of the risen Christ, Peter confesses publicly with the whole Church before the assembled peoples from all over the world: "There is salvation in no one else, for there is no other name under heaven given among mortals by which we must be saved" (Acts 4:12). If through Baptism in the name of the Father and of the Son and of the Holy Spirit (see Matt. 28:19) we have been redeemed from sin and death and have become a "new creation" (Gal. 6:15), this in no way dilutes the expected resurrection of the dead on the Last Day into some sort of myth that must be interpreted existentially.[57] Their

---

[57] Rudolf Bultmann, *Neues Testament und Mythologie. Das Problem der Entmythologisierung der neutestamentlichen Verkündigung* (1941), Munich, 1985.

resurrection brings the dead into the Christological center of their existence before God and reveals and perfects our being, all of us, sons and daughters of God in Jesus Christ. We are inserted through grace into the real relation of the Father to His coessential eternal Son and are thus, in the Spirit of the Father and the Son, adoptive children of God (cf. Rom. 8:15; Gal. 4:4-5; Eph. 1:5). Our grace-dependent relationship to God, whom we address personally in prayer as "Our Father in heaven" (Matt. 6:9; Luke 11:2), already began in the sonship of God's people Israel (see 2 Sam. 7:14; 1 Chron. 17:13; Rom. 9:4). "Why have they been numbered among the *children of God*? And why is their lot among the saints?" (Wisd. 5:5; cf. Matt. 5:9). "Indeed they cannot die any more, because they are like angels and are *children of God*, being children of the resurrection" (Luke 20:36).

If those who believe in Christ are members of the Body of Christ through Baptism and thus connected to the assumed human nature of the Son of God, then they are "also predestined to be conformed to the image of his Son, in order that he might be the firstborn within a large family [among many brothers]" (Rom. 8:29). They are predestined through, in, and with the God-Man, Jesus Christ, the Second Person of the Trinity, to participate eternally in the triune life of God, who alone "has immortality" (1 Tim. 6:16).[58]

The *Resurrection of Christ*,[59] like our *bodily resurrection*,[60] is a reality that God alone can bring about. We are saved when we hold

---

[58] Karl-Heinz Menke, *Jesus ist der Sohn Gottes. Denkformen und Brennpunkt der Christologie* (Regensburg: Pustet, 2008).

[59] Hans Kessler, *Sucht den Lebenden nicht bei den Toten. Die Auferstehung Jesu Christi in biblischer, fundamentaltheologischer und systematischer Sicht* (Würzburg: Echter, 1995).

[60] Gisbert Greshake and Jacob Kremer, *Resurrectio mortuorum. Zum theologischen Verständnis der leiblichen Auferstehung* (Darmstadt: Wissenschaftliche Buchgesellschaft, 1986).

fast in faith to the Word proclaimed to us by the apostles. The confession of the early Church is our faith: "that Christ died for our sins in accordance with the scriptures, and that he was buried, and that he was raised on the third day in accordance with the scriptures, and that he appeared to Cephas, then to the twelve" (1 Cor. 15:3-5).[61]

According to the premises of modern subject philosophy, the faith of the Christian is merely the content of his or her consciousness (the *res cogitans*) without any reference point in physical, historical reality (*res extensa*). After the dialectical opposition of grace and (totally corrupt) nature in Protestant theology rendered the path of metaphysics as a way to God and thus the synthesis of reason and faith obsolete, this led to the meaning of existence in the world as a path to God being excluded from the exact sciences. Hence, religious life can—according to the sociologist of religion Max Weber (1864-1920)—exist outside the rationally operating sciences only in the form of irrational mysticism and emotion-based religious romanticism. Science is undoubtedly a "specifically irreligious power."[62] Weber argues that even though there is no presuppositionless science, theology's invoking of the authority—as an "intellectual rationalisation of the possession of sacred values"—of presuppositions that it creates itself, such as "miracles" and "revelation," makes "the tension between the

[61] Karl Lehmann, *Auferweckt am dritten Tag. Früheste Christologie, Bekenntnisbildung und Schriftauslegung im Lichte von 1 Kor 15, 3–5* (Freiburg: Herder, 1968).

[62] Max Weber, *Vom inneren Beruf zur Wissenschaft* (1917): id., *Soziologie*, ed. J. Winckelmann (Stuttgart, 1968), 322. English: *Science as a Vocation, Cultural Apparatus*, https://culturalapparatus.wordpress.com/science-as-a-vocation-%e2%80%94-max-weber/.

value-spheres of 'science' and the sphere of 'the holy' (*des religiösen Heils*) unbridgeable."[63]

In order to venture beyond reason to faith as a pure option of theoretical reason and a postulate of practical reason[64] or as a leap[65] into the paradox that, through God's Incarnation, the eternal exists in time,[66] one can scarcely invoke Tertullian's alleged dictum "*Credo, quia absurdum.*" In his fight against the naturalization and de-historicization of Christianity in the Gnostic speculations on reason, Tertullian's concern was, in fact, not to "build" faith upon the abyss of a reason devoid of being and meaning; what mattered to him was that faith cannot be derived from the thought possibilities of limited natural reason and the measuring of the infinite against the finite. "The Son of God was crucified; I am not ashamed because men must needs be ashamed of it. And the Son of God died; it is by all means to be believed, because it is absurd. And He was buried, and rose again; the fact is certain,

---

[63] Ibid., 337.

[64] Immanuel Kant, *Kritik der reinen Vernunft* B XXX: "Ich musste also das Wissen aufheben, um zum Glauben Platz zu bekommen" (I had to deny knowledge in order to make room for faith).

[65] Gotthold Ephraim Lessing, *Über den Beweis des Geistes und der Kraft* (1777), in *Lessing's Werke III*, 311: "That, then, is the ugly broad ditch which I cannot get across" between the accidental historical truths and the metaphysical truths. It would be unreasonable "to expect me to alter all my fundamental ideas of the nature of the God-head because I cannot see any credible (historical) testimony against the resurrection of Christ." According to Aristotelian logic, this would constitute the incomprehensible change to a different conceptual sphere—the *metábasis eis állo génos* (Analytica Posteriora 75b).

[66] Sören Kierkegaard, *Philosophische Brocken*, Kap. III, Werke V (Reinbek b. Hamburg, 1967), 36-46.

because it is impossible — *Dei filius sepultus resurrexit: certum est, quia impossibile est.*"[67]

Faith as knowledge of God's infinitude cannot be rationalistically derived from finite reason; this would be a *contradictio in adjecto.* For such faith is at heart a response of surrender to the divine love that precedes it. When the believer becomes one with God in love, however, reason certainly does not find itself pushed into darkness but rather fulfilled and delighted in its striving for a knowledge of God. "No one comprehends what is truly God's except the Spirit of God. Now we have received not the spirit of the world, but the Spirit that is from God, so that we may understand the gifts bestowed on us by God.... Those who are spiritual discern all things, and they are themselves subject to no one else's scrutiny" (1 Cor. 2:11–12, 15).

Against Max Weber's justification of theology as a science according to its rational and historical method while considering it scientifically unprovable according to its dogmatic foundation, it could be argued that theology does not set its own premises in a decisionistic-optional way. Instead, it builds on the witness borne by the prophets and the apostles to Jesus, the Christ, who attest that when "the time is fulfilled" (Mark 1:15; Gal. 4:4; Eph. 1:10), He established the Kingdom of God in His Person and in history. The risen Christ, "the Word of life" (see 1 John 1:1), gave Himself to them to see, hear, and touch in the Easter appearances and, in so doing, revealed Himself to them. The apostles testify to the identity of the earthly and paschal Christ with their confession: "The Lord has risen *indeed*, and he has appeared to Simon!" (Luke 24:34). And therefore he is also *indeed* truly present under the species of bread and wine with the substance of His

---

[67] Tertullian, *De carne Christi* 5, cf. Tertullian, *De baptismo* 2.

Flesh and Blood in the midst of the community of His disciples and gives Himself to them as food and drink for eternal life. The risen Lord in the shape of the unknown wayfarer walked with the disciples on their way to Emmaus, and when they urged Him: "Stay with us" (Luke 24:29), He went into their house. "When he was at the table with them, he took bread, blessed and broke it, and gave it to them. Then their eyes were opened, and they recognized him" (Luke 24:30-31). They understood that it was He who had explained to them the meaning of the Scriptures. The crucified Lord, risen from the dead, is the same Lord who took the bread and the cup of wine in His hands in the Upper Room and said to His disciples: "This is my body, which is given for you. Do this in remembrance of me" and "This cup that is poured out for you is the new covenant in my blood" (Luke 22:19-20). With respect to the primitive form of the eucharistic memorial that emerges here, the Second Vatican Council could say: "The two parts which, in a certain sense, go to make up the Mass, namely, the liturgy of the word and the eucharistic liturgy, are so closely connected with each other that they form but one single act of worship."[68]

Jesus Himself overcomes the disciples' perfectly understandable doubts about the message of the Resurrection of One who had died on the Cross, something incomprehensible to mere (speculative and everyday practical) reason. When they think they are seeing a "spirit" (as a figment of their imagination) at the Easter apparition in Jerusalem, Jesus says: "Why are you frightened, and why do doubts arise in your hearts? Look at my hands and my feet; see that *it is I myself*. Touch me and see; for a ghost does not have flesh and bones as you see that I have" (Luke 24:38-39).

[68] Second Vatican Council, *Sacrosanctum concilium* 56.

The testimony and "teaching of the apostles" (Acts 2:42; cf. 1 Cor. 15:12, etc.) are present in the apostles' preaching and sealed with the blood of their martyrdom. The confession of the primitive Church remains present in the preaching and teaching of the Church in the apostolic succession. But the word that is proclaimed is by no means merely a reporting of far-off historical events or a reflection of inner religious moods and states of consciousness. It is much more the sacramental medium of the Word of God, who speaks to us personally and with salvific effect in the Church's preaching. The proclaimed Word of God brings about salvation only when it connects with the hearers through faith (Heb. 4:2). "The very concept of revelation requires a someone who becomes aware of it."[69]

Paul, Silvanus, and Timothy already write with apostolic authority to the Thessalonians: "We also constantly give thanks to God for this, that when you received the word of God that you heard from us, you accepted it not as a human word but as what it really is, God's word, which is also at work in you believers" (1 Thess. 2:13).

The truth of revelation does not depend on the subjectivity of the believer and is certainly not constituted by it as a phenomenon in the believer's consciousness. But it becomes effective in faith personally (subjectively) only through the inner illumination of the mind and the will by the Holy Spirit because otherwise faith would not be a personal *relationship to God* but only a "thingly disposable" (*dinglich-verfügbar*) *knowledge about God*.

The revelation in which we believe is not just the (objectively describable) content of what we believe; even more it is the (subjectively spontaneous) encounter with the personal God in the act

---

[69] Joseph Ratzinger, *Offenbarungsverständnis und Geschichtstheologie Bonaventuras*, in JRGS 2 (Freiburg i. Br: Herder, 2009), 13-659.

of His speaking to us. The combined effect of God's Word and the faith of the Church in her individual members is to raise the Christian concept of revelation above the alternative of an objectivistic, information-theoretical and a subjectivistic, consciousness-dependent approach—as was already shown by Joseph Ratzinger in his post-doctoral thesis on St. Bonaventure.[70] This also prepared the way for the Second Vatican Council's understanding of revelation. In the Dogmatic Constitution on Divine Revelation *Dei verbum* (1965), the indissoluble connection between God's revelation and human faith is explained as follows:

> In his goodness and wisdom God chose to reveal *himself* and to make known to us the hidden purpose of his will by which through Christ, the Word made flesh, man might in the Holy Spirit have access to the Father and come to share in the divine nature. Through this revelation, therefore, the invisible God out of the abundance of his love speaks to men as friends and lives among them, so that he may invite and take them into fellowship with himself.[71]

Man responds to God's self-revelation in His Word with the obedience of faith.

> "The obedience of faith is to be given to God who reveals, an obedience by which man commits his whole self freely to God, offering the full submission of intellect and will to God who reveals," and freely assenting to the truth revealed by him. To make this act of faith, the grace of God and the interior help of the Holy Spirit must precede and

---

[70] Ibid., 53–659.
[71] Second Vatican Council, *Dei verbum* 2.

assist, moving the heart and turning it to God, opening the eyes of the mind and giving "joy and ease to everyone in assenting to the truth and believing it." To bring about an ever deeper understanding of revelation the same Holy Spirit constantly brings faith to completion by his gifts.[72]

Since God is the Creator of our free will, He is not obliged—like the ideologues of all ages—to establish forcibly His kingdom and law with coercion of thought and conscience. God's greatness respects our freedom to such an extent that it even leaves room for negation of the faith. It is only the possibility of saying no to Him that makes freedom of faith possible as a personal act of surrender, trust, cognition, and lifestyle through which man, as a *cooperator Dei*, earns salvation as a reward. "See, I am coming soon; my reward is with me, to repay according to everyone's work" (Rev. 22:12). For "to believe is itself nothing but to cogitate with assent—*credere nihil aliud est, quam cum assensione cogitare*."[73]

Outside free consent, faith would not be faith, but only unwilling submission to a coercion of thought, which would necessarily destroy the personal, childlike, trusting, and friendly relationship to the God of truth, life, and love. Reason cognizes the essentialities and modes of action of material things, whereas it can grasp spiritual realities only analogously from their effects. In order to cognize the supernatural self-revelation of God in His word and work, our intellect requires a stronger source of light—the infused light of the Holy Spirit.[74]

---

[72] Ibid., 5. This fundamental magisterial document is to be read in the context of the First Vatican Council's Dogmatic Constitution on the Catholic Faith *Dei Filius* and as its continuation.

[73] Augustine, *De praedestinatione sanctorum* II, 5.

[74] Thomas Aquinas, *Summa theologiae* I, q. 88, a. 3.

God's Presence in the Eucharist and in the World

But reason can also make judgments about the true, which it acknowledges, and the false, which it rejects. In the former, faith has no evidence because it cannot grasp God and His revealed mysteries as it does the realities of the world. In the sense of the judging intellect and the decision-making will, however, the Christian arrives at a certainty of faith because he can rely on the absolutely reliable authority of the God of triune love.[75]

Faith in the ecclesial sense, however, is the recognition of a reality worked by God that goes beyond verification by the natural intellectual faculty and its categorial criteria; we become certain of it instead on account of the authority of God, revealing Himself to us in the Holy Spirit.

Jesus is *truly* risen and will also give life to our mortal bodies and grant us God's gift of eternal life.

> When this perishable body puts on imperishability, and this mortal body puts on immortality, then the saying that is written will be fulfilled:
>
> "Death has been swallowed up in victory."
> "Where, O death, is your victory?
> Where, O death, is your sting?"
>
> The sting of death is sin, and the power of sin is the law. But thanks be to God, who gives us the victory through our Lord Jesus Christ. (1 Cor. 15:54–57)

Because in our belief in the Father and the Son and the Holy Spirit we are "called children of God; and so we are" (1 John 3:1), it follows that "we have been buried with him by baptism into death, so that, just as Christ was raised from the dead by the glory

---

[75] Thomas Aquinas, *De Veritate*, q. 14, a. 1.

of the Father, so we too might walk in newness of life. For if we have been united with him in a death like his, we will certainly be united with him in a resurrection like his" (Rom. 6:4–5).

During his great speech in the synagogue of Capernaum about the "bread that came down from heaven," Jesus reveals His oneness with the Father as the source of all life. He discloses to His disciples an insight into the original unity and inner consistency of the mysteries of salvation, from the Trinity and the Incarnation to the Church and the Eucharist, and to the mystery of the resurrection of the dead and their eternal life in God. These (plural) human "words of eternal life" (John 6:68) that Jesus, the (singular) Divine "Word, Life and Light" (see John 1:4), speaks to His disciples can be grasped in all their depth and fullness only through meditating on them. These words require no theological interpretation because in them the Divine Word, Jesus Christ, the only Son "who is close to the Father's heart [bosom]" (John 1:18), directly interprets Himself (*ex-egesato*):

> And this is the will of him who sent me, that I should lose nothing of all that he has given me, but raise it up on the last day. This is indeed the will of my Father, that all who see the Son and believe in him may have eternal life; and I will raise them up on the last day.
>
> …No one can come to me unless drawn by the Father who sent me; and I will raise that person up on the last day. It is written in the prophets, "And they shall *all be taught* by God." Everyone who has heard and learned from the Father comes to me. Not that anyone has seen the Father except the one who is from God; he has seen the Father. Very truly, I tell you, whoever believes has eternal life. I am the bread of life.… *the bread that I will give for the life of the*

world is my flesh.... Those who eat my flesh and drink my blood have eternal life, and I *will* raise them up on the last day; for my flesh is true food and my blood is true drink. Those who eat my flesh and drink my blood abide in me, and I in them. Just as the living Father sent me, and I live because of the Father, so whoever eats me will live because of me.... But the one who eats this bread will live for ever. (John 6:39–58)

Chapter 10

He is the Head of
the Body, the Church

Colossians 1:18

The Church of Jesus Christ did not found and organize herself as a result of human initiatives. Rather, she was founded by God and organically constituted by Him. The Church as the Body of Christ is organically connected to Him as the body is to its head, which directs and animates it. The Church's relationship to Christ is like that of a bride to her bridegroom: "just as Christ loved the church and gave himself up for her, in order to make her holy by cleansing her with the washing of water by the word" (Eph. 5:25-26). The sole reason for the existence in the world of the Church, united from the unity of the triune God,[76] is for her to fulfill God's universal plan of salvation and to make known to mankind the eternal mystery of His love (see Rom. 16:25; Eph. 3:8). It is God's will "that through the church the wisdom of God in its rich variety might now be made known to the rulers and authorities in the heavenly places. This was in accordance with the eternal purpose that he has carried out in Christ Jesus our Lord" (Eph. 3:10-11).

So the Church is neither a secular welfare organization nor the program for a global Great Reset of self-redemption; rather, she is,

---

[76] Cf. Cyprian of Carthage, *De Oratione Domnini* 23.

in Christ, the catholic or universal sacrament of the salvation of the world: "The Church is in Christ like a sacrament or as a sign and instrument both of a very closely knit union with God and of the unity of the whole human race."[77]

In the course of salvation history, the nature and form of the Church of the triune God have emerged ever more clearly. We apprehend her as the house and people of the Father, as the Body of Christ and temple of the Holy Spirit. Due to the completion of the historical and eschatological revelation of God in the Incarnation and the saving events of the Passion, atoning death, and Resurrection of the Son of God, the *Verbum Incarnatum*, and in the outpouring of the Holy Spirit from the Father and the Son at Pentecost, the Church herself has an incarnational and sacramental form. She is animated and moved by the work of the Holy Spirit. Christ, the risen Lord and her invisible Head, continues His mission for the salvation of mankind to the end of time through the Church.

The Church, which Christ, the Son of the living God, built on the rock of Peter, is the visible and real presence of God in this world. It is the *Christus praesens* in the corporate form of the community of faith. God establishes her as a visibly constituted community of salvation and of the saints (the baptized). Through her proclamation and witness, He calls people into His community of salvation and incorporates the many individuals into His Mystical Body—*Corpus Christi Mysticum*—as members of it. "But speaking the truth in love, we must grow up in every way into him who is the head, into Christ, from whom the whole body, joined and knitted together by every ligament with which it is equipped, as each part is working properly, promotes the body's growth in building itself up in love" (Eph. 4:15-16).

---

[77] Second Vatican Council, *Lumen gentium* 1.

And the exalted Lord speaks to us through the apostolic teaching. He Himself speaks as our Teacher, acts as our Shepherd and Priest in the person of the bishops, who, in the apostolic succession, act with apostolic authority for the salvation of the faithful. Therefore, it is in and through the Church of the triune God that the presence of Jesus Christ is mediated and comes about for the salvation of the world. Through the apostles and the Church, Jesus continues His mission, which will go on until His return at the end of time. When the risen Lord revealed Himself to the disciples, He spoke the words that legitimize the Church's mission for the eternal salvation of mankind for all time: "Peace be with you. As the Father has sent me, so I send you.... Receive the Holy Spirit" (John 20:21–22).

The Church of the Triune God is therefore not merely a regionally and temporally limited form of religion. Nor is she just the culturally or ethnically bound expression of man's religious disposition to worship God, insofar as we understand by this man's natural spiritual, moral, and affective orientation toward transcendence or toward the divine horizon beyond the contingent world with its need for redemption. This would only be religion as a moral virtue such as belongs to the intellectual and moral nature of man[78] but not the supernatural worship of God through the virtues of faith, hope, and love, infused by the Holy Spirit.[79]

Jesus Christ, true God and true man, is the Mediator of creation, of the deep reconciliation and of the hoped-for perfection of man in God. As the Head of all creation, He is also the Head of the Church. He fills the Church, which is His Body, with His life (see Eph. 1:23). And this means that "through the

[78] Thomas Aquinas, *Summa theologiae* II-II, q. 81 (*de religione*).
[79] Cf. ibid., qq. 1–27.

church the wisdom of God in its rich variety might now be made known" to the whole of creation "in accordance with the eternal purpose that he has carried out in Christ Jesus our Lord" (Eph. 3:10–11). Jesus Christ is the sole and universal Mediator between God and man (see 1 Tim. 2:5–6). For God, His Father, wants all people to be saved through Him and to come to a knowledge of the truth. This is effected in the universal, or catholic, mission of "the church of the living God, the pillar and bulwark of the truth" (1 Tim. 3:15).

But an even more concrete portrayal of the Church's mission can be achieved by looking at those it addresses—namely, the people loved by God to whom the gospel message of their salvation is delivered. These are people in their own respective epoch, culture, and social order with their own mentalities, attitudes toward life, and lifestyles. The Second Vatican Council did not merely offer us an authentic view of the Church in *Lumen gentium*. With the Pastoral Constitution *Gaudium et spes*, it also looked in detail at the pastoral mission of "the Church in the modern world." The Church comes from God and in her life becomes, through the Gospel and the sacraments, the instrument of the forgiveness of sins, the sanctification and divinization of human beings, the experience of the dignity as children of God and their vocation to eternal life. However, the Church also consists of people who are united in Christ and guided by the Holy Spirit but are children of their time. With those of other faiths and nonbelievers, Christians share in the opportunities, hopes, sufferings, and decadence of their age.[80] Every age has its challenges and abysses. The Church has the duty to scrutinize the signs of the times and to interpret

---

[80] Second Vatican Council, Pastoral Council on the Church in the Modern World *Gaudium et spes* (December 7, 1965), no. 1.

them in the light of the gospel.[81] She must raise her voice prophetically, calling what is true true, what is good and also what is evil evil. The concrete visible Church is the subject of faith.

Instead of starting from transcendental philosophy or a metaphysics with a transcendental turn, or — like Ernst Troeltsch — deriving Christianity in terms of cultural theory from a general "religious a priori," or beginning with religious musicality, which, as we all know, not everyone possesses, or seeking refuge in its sense of contingency, modern Protestant theology — and this also applies mutatis mutandis to Catholic theology — should develop an "ecclesial epistemology and doctrine of principles." It is not "religion as a pious feeling" or as a "natural disposition to worship God" that is the locus of faith and the mediation of salvation but rather the Church founded by Christ, which, with Him as her Head, forms one Body. This also distinguishes the approach of theology as a science of faith from the philosophy of religion or the study of comparative religion. The community (*Gemeinschaft*) of those who believe in Christ as the Word of God made flesh and the only Mediator of salvation and truth is the bearer of the knowledge of God and the hearer of the Word. The Church is not a community (*Gemeinde*) of people sharing the same subjective sentiments and a Western or Atlantic canon of values but rather the Body of Christ. The Church is the "*Christus praesens*" — "Christ existing as the church [*Gemeinde*]."[82]

The Protestant but ecumenically open-minded theologian Dietrich Bonhoeffer (1906–1945), who became a martyr for Christ in his resistance to the godless Nazi regime, points out that Luther did not

[81] Ibid., no. 4.
[82] Dietrich Bonhoeffer, *Sanctorum Communio. Eine dogmatische Untersuchung zur Soziologie der Kirche* = DBW 1 (Munich, 1986), 126.

abolish the priesthood altogether and its service in mediating salvation but only its being exclusively bound to the ordained ministry, which he identified as a relapse into a pagan sacrificial priesthood and, in its exclusive authority to offer the sacrifice of the Mass, as an exponent of justification by works. For this seemed to him to be an intermediary agent that restricted immediacy to God in faith and love in that the Christian was bound in his encounter with God to a humanly devised system of materially mediated grace. But according to Luther's understanding of the universal priesthood, every Christian is a messenger, a witness, and thus a mediator of the Word, and in everyone who needs help or is suffering, I encounter Christ as the actual Mediator. Precisely if all her members are priests and worship God directly in faith, prayer, and service to others, the Church is not without priests and without worship.

In the Church, we do not speak of God as of a common object and project; rather, God speaks to us in her. Through the Church's preaching and witness, God speaks to all whom He wishes to call into a community of life with the Father, the Son, and the Holy Spirit. "Church is the place where God speaks, where he is there for us. Whoever passes by the church passes by God," says Bonhoeffer.[83] And because Christ is not the ideal man as such, but as the Crucified is the real man for others, the Church can be Christ's Church only if she is there for others. For "our relationship to God is no 'religious' relationship to some highest, most powerful, best being imaginable — that is no genuine transcendence. Instead, our relationship to God is a new life in 'being there for others', through participation in the being of Jesus."[84]

---

[83] Dietrich Bonhoeffer, *Gesammelte Schriften* V, 23.

[84] Dietrich Bonhoeffer, *Widerstand und Ergebung*, ed. E. Bethge (Munich: Christian Kaiser Verlag, 1970), 141; *Letters and Papers from*

Thus it follows that the relationship of man to God, which is grounded in the justification of the sinner, is an event that both brings about and presupposes the Church.

We must overcome the danger of narrowing down justification individualistically as an inner relationship of grace to God and deriving the Church only secondarily from man's natural tendency to form communities or of allowing it as a concession to the spiritually autonomous subject whose corporeal-social constitution means that he has need of a sensual visualization of salvation and the guidance of external authorities without its having any relevance for our relationship to God. But—as Bonhoeffer makes clear—we do not come to the Church because a romantic sense of community makes us feel we need it or because people with weak personalities look for support from leadership figures but rather because the Church is a reality of His grace given to us by God. The Church must not orientate herself according to "religious needs." This would not take her beyond a utilitarian and functionalistic self-justification. What could one say to someone who thinks that he can manage quite well without religion and the Church? When we confess *credo ecclesiam*, we understand the Church as a gift of God, a *donum Dei*, and not as an offer that must be geared to our requirements, like some customer advisory service.

With regard to the Catholic understanding of Church and justification, I would now like to postulate the following thesis:

The hitherto irreconcilable antithesis between Protestants and Catholics does not actually manifest itself in the concept of justification by grace alone. For it is utterly clear, from the sources of the Christian faith in the Sacred Scriptures we share, that redemption

---

Prison, trans. J. DeGruchy (Minneapolis: Augsburg Fortress Press, 2010) (SCM-Canterbury edition).

cannot be bestowed on any human being subjectively in justification resulting from his own actions, as this would then make the sinner, as it were, his or her own redeemer.

The still unresolved contrast lies not in the existence and nature of the Church but rather in the significance of her visible, institutional form and her necessity for the mediation of salvation. The questions of the sacraments, the priesthood, and the teaching authority of the pope and the college of bishops merely follow logically from this.

For Luther, the Church is, in a nutshell, a *creatura verbi*:

> But the Church owes its life to the word of promise through faith, and is nourished and preserved by this same word. That is to say, the promises of God make the Church, not the Church the promise of God. For the Word of God is incomparably superior to the Church, and in this Word the Church, being a creature, has nothing to decree, ordain or make, but only to be decreed, ordained and made.[85]

What this means is that the inner Church as the congregation of saints, the justified whom God alone knows, is formed through the word of promise in faith but is present and manifests itself only where word and sacrament are preached and administered in accordance with their foundation.[86] It is a somewhat different matter if the external Church order is regulated by the secular

---

[85] Martin Luther, Von der babylonischen Gefangenschaft der Kirche (De captivitate babylonica), in WA 6, 560–561. English: *On the Babylonian Captivity of the Church*, trans. A. T. W. Steinhäuser, revised by Frederick C. Ahrens and Abdel Ross Wentz, On the Wing, http://www.onthewing.org/user/Luther%20-%20Babylonian%20Captivity.pdf.
[86] Confessio Augustana 7.

authorities or by the members of an organization. This institutional belonging to a corporate body has no salvific relevance for justification and thus for membership of the Church in the true and proper sense—namely, of the Church as the *communio sanctorum*, i.e., those truly justified in faith who are known to God alone. But visibility is considerably more than the outward organizational framework when the preaching of the gospel and the offering of the sacraments is combined in a mutual constitution with the "one holy Church" that "is to continue forever"—namely, "the congregation of saints and true believers, in which the Gospel is rightly taught and the Sacraments are rightly administered."[87]

The Catholic view of the Church proceeds from the opposite understanding—namely, that we can achieve salvific community only through and in the visible Church with her authoritative teaching and sacramental means of salvation and by recognizing her apostolic constitution and order as established by Christ in the Holy Spirit.

Johann Adam Möhler (1796-1838), the most profound thinker of the Catholic Tübingen School, sums up the difference in his *Symbolik*: "The Catholics teach: the visible Church is first, then comes the invisible one: it is the former that produces the latter. The Lutherans, however, say the opposite: the visible comes out of the invisible, and the latter is the reason for the former. This seemingly extremely insignificant antithesis expresses an enormous difference."[88]

---

[87] Ibid., 7-8.

[88] Johann Adam Möhler, *Symbolik oder Darstellung der dogmatischen Gegensätze der Katholiken und Protestanten nach ihren öffentlichen Bekenntnisschriften*, § 48, ed. J. R. Geiselmann (Cologne and Olten, 1958), 482-483. English: *Symbolism, or Exposition of the Doctrinal Differences* (New York: Edward Dunigan, 1844).

God's Presence in the Eucharist and in the World

According to Möhler, Luther's understanding of the Church is not utterly wrong, just one-sided. It therefore does not have to be rejected in toto and can also be deemed a corrective to a Catholic ecclesiology committed one-sidedly to the visible form of the Church.

In order not to make assurance of salvation dependent on created things and people in the Church, Luther rejects the salvific efficacy of the sacraments *ex opere operato*, the binding nature and infallibility of the decisions of Church councils, and the spiritual authority of the priest consecrated in his ordination (*character indelebilis*) to offer the Sacrifice of the Mass. For in all of them he sees the danger of man's putting himself in a right relationship to God through human works and institutions instead of through faith. But for him, nothing created can ever be the ground of the justification of a sinner; it can only be the ground of the place and space in which it is manifested in keeping with man's physical nature. The visible serves only as a reassurance of what takes place on the level of the immediacy between God and man in the correlation of God's promise and grace-effected faith.

From the Catholic point of view, however, this fails to value sufficiently the fundamental law of the mediation of grace, which is grounded in the Incarnation and says that on account of our physical, social, and historical constitution, we can reach the invisible only via the visible, *per visibilia ad invisibilia*.

It is certainly true to say with Luther that the means of grace of the Church and the Church as a medium of salvation are not and cannot be in themselves the cause of salvation. But even three hundred years before him, Thomas Aquinas already stated that the sacraments do not cause salvation *principaliter et effective*, but merely instrumentally transmit to the recipient the salvation that happened once and for all. "And, consequently, Christ alone is the perfect

Mediator of God and men, inasmuch as, by His death, He reconciled the human race to God."[89] And with respect to the sacramentally ordained bishops and presbyters, he says: "As to the priests of the New Law, they may be called mediators of God and men, inasmuch as they are the ministers of the true Mediator by administering, in His stead, the saving sacraments to men (*vice ipsius*)."[90] And the Sacrifice of the Mass is not different from the Sacrifice of the Cross, but as the *Memoriale Dominicae Passionis*, it is the sacramental representation of Jesus' life and His death on the Cross for mankind.[91]

Even when it comes to the question of whether the pope has gone so far as to put himself in the place of Christ and, in so doing, assumed the features of the antichrist, which became the major bone of contention in the controversy between Reformers and Catholics, the contrast is not as clear-cut as it seems. To the question of whether Christ alone is the rock and foundation of the Church, and why, despite this, Simon Bar-Jonah is also called Rock and Petros or Cephas, Thomas Aquinas answers in his commentary on the Gospel of Matthew:

> Christ is it in himself: Rock and foundation of the Church. The apostles are it not in themselves, but by the imposition of Christ and the authority given to them by Christ. And this is especially true of Peter's house, which was founded on rock, lest it fall down, as with the wise man who built his house on rock rather than on sand. The Church can be fought, but not beaten down.[92]

---

[89] Thomas Aquinas, *Summa theologiae* III, q. 26 a. 1; cf. *Summa theologiae* I-II, q. 112, ad 2.

[90] Thomas Aquinas, *Summa theologiae* III, q. 26, a. 1, ad 1.

[91] Ibid., q. 79, a. 7.

[92] Thomas Aquinas, *Comment in Ev. Matt.*, ad cap. 16, 17.

God's Presence in the Eucharist and in the World

The devaluation of the sacraments that occurs in an idealized and spiritualized Christianity must be countered with the argument that the sacraments are not merely pedagogically useful for those who are still immature in the faith. Rather, they correspond to our human nature in its substantial unity of body and soul. They are also positively grounded in the Incarnation and in God's entire plan of salvation. Christ entrusted the sacraments to the apostles, their successors, and the whole Church to administer, and in the Holy Spirit, He gives them the supernatural effect that fundamentally distinguishes them from arbitrary religious symbols. The sacraments are not just signs; they are *effective signs*, effective through the action of Christ and fruitful in faith and love. Luther, too, is aware of the objective efficacy of Baptism, as becomes clear at least in his retention of infant Baptism. And Philip Melanchthon justifies this with the anti-Donatist decision that the sacraments that are administered by an unworthy person are valid (*sacramenta efficacia*).[93]

In his essay "The Eternal Significance of Jesus' Humanity," Karl Rahner has shown that the dialectical opposition between man's immediacy to God and ecclesial and sacramental mediation is removed in the hypostatic union in that both the unity and the difference of divine and human nature, and thus of immediacy and mediation, are grounded in the person of the *Verbum Incarnatum*:

> Jesus, the man, not merely *was* at one time of decisive importance for our salvation, that is, for the real finding of the absolute God, by his historical and now past acts of the cross, and the like, but—as the one who became man and has remained a creature—he is *now* and for all eternity

---

[93] *Confessio Augustana* 8.

the *permanent openness* of our finite being to the living God of infinite, eternal life; he is, therefore, even in his humanity the created reality for us which stands in the act of our religion in such a way that, without this act toward his humanity and through it (implicitly or explicitly), the basic religious act toward God could never reach its goal.

One always sees the Father only through Jesus. Just as *im*-mediately as this, for the directness of the vision of God is not a denial of the mediatorship of Christ as man.[94]

Or expressed unsurpassably in Jesus' own words: "Whoever has seen me has seen the Father" (John 14:9; cf. 12:45).

Church as *creatura verbi* and Church as *sacramentum salutis mundi* are two starting points that have so far proved to be somewhat incompatible, but this may not necessarily have to be the case. If, for example, the visible and invisible Church, divine salvation and the mediation entrusted to human beings are not set dialectically against one another but rather related analogously to each other in the light of the mystery of the Incarnation—showing what connects and what distinguishes them—then it is possible to follow Vatican II in taking up Luther's concern and nevertheless expressing the Catholic Faith in a way that is free from any pointedly controversial theological emphasis:

[94] Karl Rahner, *Die ewige Bedeutung der Menschheit Jesu für unser Gottes-verhältnis*, in Karl Rahner, *Menschsein und Menschwerdung Gottes. Studien zur Grundlegung der Dogmatik, zur Christologie, Theologischen Anthropologie und Eschatologie* (= Sämtliche Werke 12) (Freiburg i. Br.: Herder, 2005), 258. English translation from Karl Rahner, *The Content of Faith: The Best of Karl Rahner's Theological Writings*, ed. Karl Lehmann and Albert Raffelt, trans. edited by Harvey D. Egan, S.J. (New York: Crossroad Publishing, 1933; repr. 2000), 331-332.

Christ, the one Mediator, established and continually sustains here on earth his holy Church, the community of faith, hope and charity, as an entity with visible delineation through which he communicated truth and grace to all. But, the society structured with hierarchical organs and the Mystical Body of Christ, are not to be considered as two realities, nor are the visible assembly and the spiritual community, nor the earthly Church and the Church enriched with heavenly things; rather they form one complex reality which coalesces from a divine and a human element.

For this reason, by no weak analogy, it is compared to the mystery of the incarnate Word. As the assumed nature, inseparably united to him, serves the divine Word as a living organ of salvation, so, in a similar way, does the visible social structure of the Church serve the Spirit of Christ, who vivifies it, in the building up of the body (cf. Eph 4:16).[95]

With regard to those Christians who, through no fault of their own, do not belong fully to the Catholic Church, Vatican II explicitly refrains from denying their gracious unity with Christ in faith, hope, and love and, despite the differences in the understanding and scope of the means of salvation, also accords the other ecclesial communities the rank of being media of salvation.[96] Therefore, on the level of visibility, too, especially in the Sacrament of Baptism, there still exists a unity of the Church and a visible communion of Christians with one another as members of the one Body of Christ even though the *communio* is not complete but is still aiming toward full visible unity in the sacramental Church.

---

[95] Second Vatican Council, *Lumen gentium* 8.
[96] Second Vatican Council, *Unitatis redintegratio* 3.

The Catholic understanding of ecumenism neither sets its sights on a restoration of the status quo ante 1520, nor can it accept the paradigm of a necessary process of pluralization in intellectual history that espouses the status quo of institutionally and confessionally different churchdoms. For the latter would be a diametrical contradiction of the will of Christ, in whom the oneness, holiness, catholicity, and apostolicity of the Church, whose Head He is, is permanently grounded. The goal of Catholic ecumenism is therefore not one of reconciled difference, but rather one of reconciling the contrasts in a deeper communion in Christ: *Unus et totus Christus, caput et membra.* After gratefully recalling the manifold bonds of unity with the non-Catholic churches, the Council continues:

> In all of Christ's disciples the Spirit arouses the desire to be peacefully united, in the manner determined by Christ, as one flock under one shepherd, and he prompts them to pursue this end. Mother Church never ceases to pray, hope and work that this may come about. She exhorts her children to purification and renewal so that the sign of Christ may shine more brightly over the face of the earth.[97]

After being divided for many centuries by the denominational polemics with their entrenched feelings of resentment, and often also misinterpretations of the respective doctrines, we must today be on our guard against falling prey to relativism and indifferentism in questions of the truth of the doctrines of the Faith and the right understanding of the Church and the sacraments. We must not make it too easy for ourselves and reduce the substantial differences in the doctrine of the Faith, ethics, and the sacramental

---

[97] Second Vatican Council, *Lumen gentium* 15.

constitution of the Church to pithy formulas or declare them to be unimportant. Christian faith is a person's total surrender of himself to God. Christianity must not be reduced to its usefulness for a politically desired civil religion. When Jesus invites all people to the wedding feast in the kingdom of God, we should not offer them the cultural and moral leftovers from the separated denominations but rather set the table of truth and offer Christ as the bread of God "which comes down from heaven and gives life to the world" (John 6:33).

What we have in common and what binds us together is not just a few values of the Christian West or the West in general, but rather the central mysteries of the revelation of salvation history: the Trinity of God, the Incarnation of the Divine Logos, the eschatological outpouring of the Holy Spirit, the belief in Christ, the reality and efficacy of grace, the forgiveness of sins, the baptized as sons and daughters of God, the hope of the resurrection of the flesh and eternal life, love of God and neighbor as the fulfillment of all the commandments, Sacred Scripture and the Apostolic Tradition of undivided Christianity, and Baptism, through which we become God's children and friends and are incorporated as members into the Body of Christ, which is the Church. All this we share—and this can be taken as the starting point for our efforts to overcome the differences in our understanding of the other sacraments, the Eucharist, the episcopate, and the Roman Petrine ministry at least to the extent that they no longer divide us in the confession of faith and ecclesial communion.

What God expects of us and what we Christians owe to humanity today is a common testimony to "the unity of the faith and of the knowledge of the Son of God, to maturity, to the measure of the full stature of Christ" (Eph. 4:13).

Chapter 11

In the world you face
persecution, but take courage
John 16:33

And remember, I am
with you always
Matthew 28:20

It is not true that people today no longer ask about the merciful God. They merely express the basic questions of success or failure differently: "What is man? What is this sense of sorrow, of evil, of death ...? What can man offer to society, what can he expect from it? What follows this earthly life?"[98]

We do not respond to these questions with self-devised world theories, therapy proposals, and social programs but with the profession of faith that comes from God and leads to God. And this is—as expressed by the Fathers of the Second Vatican Council—our common answer based on the gospel of justification through belief in Jesus the Christ:

> The Church firmly believes that Christ, who died and was raised up for all, can through his Spirit offer man the light and the strength to measure up to his supreme destiny. Nor has any other name under the heaven been given to man by which it is fitting for him to be saved. She likewise holds that in her most benign Lord and Master can be found the key, the focal point and the goal of man, as well as of all human history.[99]

---

[98] Second Vatican Council, *Gaudium et spes* 10.
[99] Ibid.

God's Presence in the Eucharist and in the World

On the other hand, since the French and Soviet Revolutions, there has been a well-financed program for the dechristianization of Europe. The goal is the creation of the new human being in the liberal cult of progress, in the political doctrines of salvation peddled in the twentieth century by fascism and communism and the reduction of man to a complex organism bereft of any spiritual-corporeal nature referenced to transcendence. The theories are called monistic materialism, positivism, or immanentism; their effect is banal and downward in their corrupting people through sensual pleasure (drugs and sex). The intention is for a scientistic-political media project to raise the relativism of truth and the denial of transcendence that are part of this interpretation of the world into a universal paradigm. In the face of this totalitarian claim to validity on the part of naturalism, global religious interpretations are accorded no more than marginal and private validity—similar to the way in which the Native Americans who remained were no longer exterminated in the name of a purportedly superior culture but nevertheless were isolated on reservations. Christianity—so the proponents of such theories assure themselves with an air of authority—has no more than historical significance and belongs in the museum of religious history.

But the Church defends not only herself against the totalitarian grab at man on the pretext of forcing happiness on him according to the ideological notions of scientists, politicians, and economists; she also defends the individual and social freedom of religion and conscience of all human beings. The Church is the advocate of freedom, which is anchored in man's spiritual-moral nature and is not his because it has been ascribed to him or denied him by parliamentary majorities or leaders of public opinion.

And man's freedom, his spiritual convictions, and his moral attitudes cannot just be factually and positivistically manipulated and standardized by a human institution—such as the state, the education system, or the administration of justice. A state law is not legitimate simply because it is formally correct but rather because it builds on justice and aims to help justice prevail. Constitutional democracy has come to a sorry pass when a doctor suffers professional disadvantages just because he refuses to kill a human being in the womb, which he firmly believes to be a crime. And since we are convinced that the bipolarity of man and woman are constitutive for marriage and a family and that no child shall be robbed of his natural right to have a father and mother of his own, things are in a very bad way when a Catholic adoption agency is closed down because it does not hand over children to just any couple or group of people.

The motto of secularism, "religion is a private matter," is a brutal violation of human rights, and furthermore of reason, since all man's essential acts accord with his communal nature and are correspondingly public. Ever since the Enlightenment and the French Revolution, so-called liberals and anticlericals have time and again justified their serious violations of the law against the Catholic Church—even going as far as the open persecution of Christians—by claiming to possess superior insight. On the other hand, a state whose task it is to attend to people's temporal concerns in a plural society must not subscribe to any specific religion or an anti-religion and an atheistic anthropology but must remain ideologically neutral while also promoting all the initiatives undertaken by religious and nonreligious communities for the sake of the common good.

Although the Church also requires human means in order to fulfill her mission, she lays no claim to political power and media glitz in society but asks only for the freedom to carry out her God-given mission for the salvation of mankind. For individual and communal freedom of religion, the public practice of religion and the ability to act according to one's own conscience both in public and in the institutions of the state—which cannot have fallen prey to and be in the hands of secularists and anticlericalists, with their arrogant belief in their own superiority—are fundamental human rights and form the basis for all peaceful coexistence in a society that contains people holding different fundamental convictions. The Church, together with other social groups, must defend freedom of religion and conscience against the state or a totalitarian ideology on the basis of natural moral law.

> On his part, man perceives and acknowledges the imperatives of the divine law through the mediation of conscience. In all his activity a man is bound to follow his conscience in order that he may come to God, the end and purpose of life. It follows that he is not to be forced to act in a manner contrary to his conscience. Nor, on the other hand, is he to be restrained from acting in accordance with his conscience, especially in matters religious. The reason is that the exercise of religion, of its very nature, consists before all else in those internal, voluntary and free acts whereby man sets the course of his life directly toward God. No merely human power can either command or prohibit acts of this kind. The social nature of man, however, itself requires that he should give external expression to his internal acts of religion: that he should share with others in matters religious; that he should profess his religion in community. Injury therefore is done to the human person and to the very order established by God for human life, if the free exercise of religion is denied in society, provided just public order is observed.

There is a further consideration. The religious acts whereby men, in private and in public and out of a sense of personal conviction, direct their lives to God transcend by their very nature the order of terrestrial and temporal affairs. Government therefore ought indeed to take account of the religious life of the citizenry and show it favour, since the function of government is to make provision for the common welfare. However, it would clearly transgress the limits set to its power, were it to presume to command or inhibit acts that are religious.[100]

In social pluralism, the Church is an advocate of humanity. In his encyclical *Pacem in terris* (1963), Pope John XXIII presented his own charter of human rights, which far surpasses the *Universal Declaration of Human Rights* (1948) of the United Nations. Man is person. That is the linchpin of his inviolable dignity. In this way, the Church overcomes precisely the horizontal framework of justification, which can change quickly at any time, and leads the discussion to the actual heart of the matter: endowed with reason and free will, the person has rights and duties that are inherent to him or her by nature. Unconditional respect for the person, for the life and limb of one's fellow human being must be accepted by all as a common basis for their actions. Then there is a real chance that the inequalities in how the earth's resources are shared will vanish and that freedom will apply to everyone and become the fundamental element supporting all social orders:

Any well-regulated and productive association of men in society demands the acceptance of one fundamental

[100] Second Vatican Council, Declaration on Religious Freedom *Dignitatis humanae* (December 7, 1965), no. 3.

principle: that each individual man is truly a person. His is a nature, that is, endowed with intelligence and free will. As such he has rights and duties, which together flow as a direct consequence from his nature. These rights and duties are universal and inviolable, and therefore altogether inalienable.[101]

The basic idea of human rights not only corresponds profoundly to the biblical-Christian understanding of mankind but is the root from which all initiatives spring to promote a high regard for human life.

The shaping of human rights is deeply linked to the teaching of the Church. In the Pastoral Constitution *Gaudium et spes*, for example, the Second Vatican Council offered its own interpretation of human rights:

> The Church, therefore, by virtue of the gospel committed to her, proclaims the rights of man; she acknowledges and greatly esteems the dynamic movements of today by which these rights are everywhere fostered. Yet these movements must be penetrated by the spirit of the gospel and protected against any kind of false autonomy. For we are tempted to think that our personal rights are fully ensured only when we are exempt from every requirement of divine law. But this way lies not the maintenance of the dignity of the human person, but its annihilation.[102]

Human rights are therefore not rules constructed by a community of a number of states but can be discerned and placed

[101] John XXIII, Encyclical *Pacem in terris* (April 11, 1963), no. 9.
[102] Second Vatican Council, *Gaudium et spes* 41.

permanently before society as a binding norm only if they are linked to God. Human rights based on the position of a political ideology are relative because they can at any time be interpreted and implemented differently by those in power. Anchoring them in God removes them from the grasp and arbitrariness of man. It is only when a higher authority is acknowledged that man is no longer at the mercy of man or trapped in the gilded cage of a neoliberal and capital-socialist "Paradise" on earth.

One of the greatest challenges facing the Church in the twenty-first century is undoubtedly the protection of human life in all stages of its development. The Church is the only community that has always faced up to this task and, in her social teaching and moral theology, stressed the value of the life of every human being.

That is why we must not tire of focusing over and over again on the human being as a person with his or her own dignity and rights. The ideological relativism that wishes to relinquish ultimately binding truth and a normative authority for moral behavior in favor of a pseudo-tolerance and seeks to eliminate the question of God by means of aggressive atheism is, in fact, engaged first and foremost in a fight against man himself.

The culture-war mentality of posthumanism claims that spirit or intellect and freedom are merely epiphenomena and functions of the neurons of the brain and the organism's genes. God is derided as a fictive moralizing and therefore inhuman penal authority. Without God, man is free and independent, no bounds can restrain him, not even the freedom of the other. In truth, however, the loss of God means that man is degraded into mere biological processes, lacking freedom of will, consideration for others, and permanently valid ethical standards. What is today considered the latest fashion may tomorrow be ridiculed as yesterday's news.

God's Presence in the Eucharist and in the World

In principle, the only solution is to focus on the human being. Man as a bodily-spiritual being is more than the sum of his biological and chemical components and his social conditioning; he is more than an animal on two legs; freedom itself releases him into being responsible for a meaningful and successful life. It is therefore crucial to emphasize the human being as a creature of God, as a person in relation to the personal God of triune love, as an individual in community with his or her own dignity and rights. For this, the fundamental Christian understanding of man's spiritual-bodily and social nature is the fundamental point of reference.

Thus, at the center of Christian anthropology is not just the isolated person as such but rather the person in community, of which the family is the primal form. Hence, the family must be protected as the space in which every human being is lovingly accepted and matures into a person who can develop in self-giving, in willingness to sacrifice, in being with and being there for others and thus reflexively finding him- or herself. The family is the "natural place for becoming human." Christian anthropology does not lose itself in vague speculation but has its concrete starting points and insights—which we often fail to notice until they are dismissed and denied. Rather, Christian anthropology is about understanding the freedom that lies in accepting the commandments established by God in man's nature as sure paths to perfection in love. Only when we have recognized that we are called to love can we properly use the freedom that has been given to us and made our responsibility. It is not freedom when we use it to set ourselves apart; rather, freedom exists when we use it for good because this lets our humanity shine forth with the light of being referenced to God as the origin and goal of all being.

It is the task of the Church to set this "Gospel of life" (John Paul II) against the anti-culture of death and to overcome the threats to the human person, to his greatness and preciousness, by proclaiming the Good News.

> The Gospel of God's love for man, the Gospel of the dignity of the person and the Gospel of life are a single and indivisible Gospel.
>
> For this reason, man — living man — represents the primary and fundamental way for the Church.[103]
>
> Every individual, precisely by reason of the mystery of the Word of God who was made flesh, is entrusted to the maternal care of the Church. Therefore every threat to human dignity and life must necessarily be felt in the Church's very heart; it cannot but affect her at the core of her faith in the Redemptive Incarnation of the Son of God, and engage her in her mission of proclaiming the Gospel of life in all the world and to every creature.[104]

Because our contemporaries are, just like us Christians, God's creatures and beloved children, we must not withhold the gospel from them. The mystery of man, the world, and history becomes clear to us only in the light of the Word made flesh — namely, in Jesus Christ. In Him we experience our divine calling to be children and friends of God, to the resurrection of the flesh, and to eternal life; and at the same time, we understand in Him our responsibility toward our neighbor and the world.

Fully aware of the complex global situation of the world and on the basis of a clear analysis of the opportunities and crises facing contemporary mankind in the history of ideas and in the sphere of politics and economics, the Second Vatican Council outlines first

---

[103] John Paul II, Encyclical *Evangelium vitae* (March 25, 1995), no. 2.
[104] Ibid., 3.

the questions and then the mission of the Church in a pluralistic society as follows:

> What does the Church think of man? What needs to be recommended for the upbuilding of contemporary society? What is the ultimate significance of human activity throughout the world? People are waiting for an answer to these questions. From the answers it will be increasingly clear that the people of God and the human race in whose midst it lives render service to each other. Thus the mission of the Church will show its religious and, by that very fact, its supremely human character.[105]

[105] Second Vatican Council, *Gaudium et spes* 11.

Chapter 12

I will give you shepherds
after my own heart

Jeremiah 3:15

Jesus Christ, the Son of the Father, is, as Head of the new humanity and of the Church, the High Priest of the New and Eternal Covenant. A synonym for the High Priest who shed His blood to atone for our sins (see Heb. 13:12) is the "great shepherd of the sheep," whom God "brought back from the dead ... by the blood of the eternal covenant" (Heb. 13:20). Jesus, the Son of the Father, reveals to His disciples the mystery of His person and mission: "I am the good shepherd. The good shepherd lays down his life for the sheep" (John 10:11). Since the Word was with God and the Son of the Father is God, in Him God fulfills His promise to Himself that He Himself will be the sole Shepherd who takes care of His people (see Ezek. 34:11–16). The apostle Peter wrote to the Christians of his time: "For you were going astray like sheep, but now you have returned to the shepherd and guardian of your souls" (1 Pet. 2:25). It is Jesus, the Son of God, who through the Incarnation took on flesh and blood in the same way as we do (cf. Heb. 2:14), of whom it is said: "Therefore he had to become like his brothers in every respect, so that he might be a merciful and faithful high priest in the service of God, to make a sacrifice of atonement for the sins of the people" (Heb. 2:17). This means that "we do not have a high priest who is unable to sympathize with our weaknesses" (Heb. 4:15) but rather one of whom it is said during His earthly ministry: "he saw a great crowd; and he had compassion for them, because they were like sheep without a shepherd" (Mark 6:34).

He appointed the apostles and, in them, their successors in the offices of bishops and presbyters to continue His mission in His name as teachers, priests, and shepherds in the Church. To all of the apostles Jesus said in a post-paschal appearance: " 'Peace be with you. As the Father has sent me, so I send you.' When he had said this, he breathed on them and said to them, 'Receive the Holy Spirit. If you forgive the sins of any, they are forgiven them; if you retain the sins of any, they are retained'" (John 20:21-23). And to Simon Peter the resurrected Lord says three times: "Feed my lambs," "Tend my sheep," "Feed my sheep" (John 21:15-17).

Without, in this context, going into the later differentiation of the apostolic ministry into the degrees of bishop and presbyter, the Apostle portrays the essence of the office of bishop and priest as a pastoral office in the sense of the self-giving of Christ, the Good Shepherd and the High Priest of the New Covenant.

To the priests appointed by the apostles Paul says: "Keep watch over yourselves and over all the flock, of which the Holy Spirit has made you overseers, to shepherd the church of God that he obtained with his own blood" (Acts 20:28). And the apostle Peter, "as an elder myself and a witness of the sufferings of Christ," exhorts the presbyters "to tend the flock of God that is in your charge, exercising the oversight, not under compulsion but willingly, as God would have you do it—not for sordid gain but eagerly. Do not lord it over those in your charge, but be examples to the flock. And when the chief shepherd appears, you will win the crown of glory that never fades away" (1 Pet. 5:1-4).

If Catholic bishops and priests understand the dignity of their vocation as the sacrifice of their lives in the service of "God the only Son, who is close to the Father's heart" (John 1:18) and whose human heart was opened on the Cross for the salvation of the world, then their self-giving devotion will become a blessing for the people. For with them God fulfills His promise: "I will give you shepherds after my own heart" (Jer. 3:15).

Vatican II gives us a brief summary of the Church's teaching on the sacramental ordained ministry:

Christ, whom the Father has sanctified and sent into the world (Jn 10:36), has through his apostles, made their successors, the bishops, partakers of his consecration and his mission. They have legitimately handed on to different individuals in the Church various degrees of participation in this ministry. Thus the divinely established ecclesiastical ministry is exercised on different levels by those who from antiquity have been called bishops, priests and deacons. Priests, although they do not possess the highest degree of the priesthood, and although they are dependent on the bishops in the exercise of their power, nevertheless are united with the bishops in sacerdotal dignity. By the power of the sacrament of orders, in the image of Christ the eternal High Priest (Heb 5:1–10; 7:24; 9:11–28), they are consecrated to preach the gospel and shepherd the faithful and to celebrate divine worship, so that they are true priests of the New Testament. Partakers of the function of Christ the sole Mediator (1 Tim 2:5), on their level of ministry, they announce the divine word to all. They exercise their sacred function especially in the eucharistic worship or the celebration of the Mass by which acting in the person of Christ and proclaiming his Mystery they unite the prayers of the faithful with the sacrifice of their Head and renew and apply in the Sacrifice of the Mass until the coming of the Lord (1 Cor 11:26) the only sacrifice of the New Testament, namely, that of Christ offering himself once for all a spotless Victim to the Father (Heb 9:11-28). For the sick and the sinners among the faithful, they exercise in the highest degree the ministry of alleviation and reconciliation, and they present the needs and the prayers of the faithful to God the Father (Heb 5:1-4). Exercising within the limits of their authority the function of Christ as Shepherd and Head, they gather together God's family as a brotherhood all of one mind, and lead them in the Spirit, through Christ, to God the Father. In the midst of the flock they adore him in spirit and in truth (Jn 4:24). Finally, they labour in word and doctrine (1 Tim 5:17), believing what they have read and meditated upon in the law of God, teaching what they have believed, and putting in practice in their own lives what they have taught.[106]

According to Thomas Aquinas, the essential element of being a Christian must be seen to lie in friendship with God. The fundamental task of the Church, which is founded on faith and the sacraments, is to serve the communion of the people with God. The Church's proclamation, sacraments, and ministries are means and instruments for a Christian life in and with God. The sacraments mediate, in the power of the Holy Spirit, communion with God. The Eucharist is supreme among the sacraments and therefore the focus and high point of Church life. All the other

---

[106] Second Vatican Council, *Lumen gentium* 28.

sacraments are ordered to it. And it is from it, too, that the epis-copacy is to be understood.

Thomas Aquinas relates the office of bishop and priest to the Lord's command to Peter: "Feed my sheep" (John 21:17). Again and again, he cites the image of the good shepherd who lays down his life for his sheep (see John 10:11). To be the shepherd of the flock entrusted to him is the main purpose and the goal of the episcopal office. The bishop or priest is commissioned to minister to the salvation of the faithful. In this, he follows Jesus Christ, who is the man for others and lays down His life for the many (see Mark 10:45). The leadership ministry assigned to the bishop is a pastoral ministry for the building up of the Church.

Both humanly and as a Christian, it is possible to carry out the consuming ministry of a priest only if you possess the necessary serenity. For this reason, the Church leader must not let the burden of his pastoral office make him neglect the joy of truth that flows from prayer and meditation. It is not the busy episcopal pastoral manager that Thomas Aquinas has in mind. Rather, he expects pastors, despite all their work of pastoral care—indeed, precisely for the sake of this pastoral care—to find enough time for study and a contemplative life. Only in this way can they do justice to the ministry of proclamation with which they are entrusted and be to the people "workers with you for your joy" (2 Cor. 1:24).

Church is realized in the celebration of the Eucharist, in which the word of proclamation also becomes present. This involves, first of all, the local aspect. The Eucharist is celebrated in a concrete place with the people who live there. There it is that the process of gathering the People of God begins. The Church is not a club of friends in which people who share a fondness for similar things get together. God's call is addressed to all people. The Church of the first centuries wanted from the start to be public in a similar way to the state itself because she is the new People of God to which all are called. That is why all the believers living in one place belong to the same Eucharist: rich and poor, educated and uneducated, Jews and Gentiles, women and men. Where Christ calls, these differences no longer count (see Gal. 3:28).

It is only in this light that it possible to understand why the martyr-bishop Ignatius of Antioch († ca. 110) linked Church membership so emphatically to being in communion with the bishop. The bishop defends the unity of the Faith against any forming of groups and any division into races and classes. The bishop of a diocese stands for the Church's being one for all since God is one for all. To this extent, the Church always has an enormous task of reconciliation to fulfill. It is only from the love of the One who died for all that this reconciliation can take place. The Letter to the Ephesians (2:14) sees the most profound significance of Christ's death as lying in the fact that He "has broken down the dividing wall, that is, the hostility between us."

It is not possible in the Eucharist to drink the Blood of Christ "poured out for many" by withdrawing into the circle of the "few." The Eucharist is the liturgy of the whole Christ, Head and Body. Reconciliation with God, which is offered to us in it, always presupposes reconciliation with our fellow human beings (see Matt. 5:23-24).

The eucharistic existence of the Church points us, first of all, to the local assembly of the People of God. The episcopal office belongs essentially to the Eucharist—as a service to unity, which necessarily follows from the sacrificial and reconciliatory character of the Eucharist. A eucharistically understood Church is—according to Ignatius of Antioch—an episcopally constituted Church.

Anyone who becomes more closely acquainted with the day-to-day life of the Church in the first centuries will recognize that it was never a matter of various local churches existing side by side. From the beginning, diverse forms of realized catholicity were an essential part of the Church. In apostolic times, it is, above all, the apostles themselves who stand outside the local principle. The apostle is not the bishop of a community but rather a missionary for the whole Church. In his person, he expresses the universal Church. No local church can claim him for itself alone. Paul carried out his mission to promote unity through his letters and through a network of messengers. These letters constitute a practiced ministry of unity that can be explained only on the basis of the Apostle's universal authority within the Church.

In the Apostolic Age, the catholic element in the structure of the Church is clear to see. The universally oriented office takes precedence over local offices. When this is understood, it also becomes possible to understand the full implications of the statement that the bishops are the successors of the apostles.

In the first phase of the Church, the bishops, as bearers of local ecclesial responsibility, were clearly under the universal ecclesial authority of the apostles with Peter at their head. The fact that, as the post-apostolic Church took shape, they were also granted the place of the apostles means that they now took on a responsibility extending beyond the local. But even in the new situation, the missionary flame must not be allowed to go out. The Church cannot be a mere collection of coexisting and, in principle, self-sufficient local churches. She must remain apostolic and missionary. The dynamic of unity shapes her entire structure.

In the second century, Irenaeus of Lyons stated emphatically:

> The Church, having received this preaching and this faith, although scattered throughout the whole world, yet, as if occupying but one house, carefully preserves it. She also

believes these points [of doctrine] just as if she had but one soul, and one and the same heart, and she proclaims them, and teaches them, and hands them down, with perfect harmony, as if she possessed only one mouth. For, although the languages of the world are dissimilar, yet the import of the tradition is one and the same. For the Churches which have been planted in Germany do not believe or hand down anything different, nor do those in Spain, nor those in Gaul, nor those in the East.... But as the sun, that creature of God, is one and the same throughout the whole world, so also the preaching of the truth shines everywhere, and enlightens all men that are willing to come to a knowledge of the truth. Nor will any one of the rulers in the Churches, however highly gifted he may be in point of eloquence, teach doctrines different from these (for no one is greater than the Master—Mt 10:24); nor, on the other hand, will he who is deficient in power of expression inflict injury on the tradition.[107]

The bishop is the link of catholicity (*catholic* literally means "relating to the whole"). He maintains the connection with the other local churches, thus embodying the apostolic and catholic element in the Church. This is already expressed in his consecration. The bishop is consecrated by a group of at least three neighboring bishops. No congregation can simply give itself its bishop. We did not produce the faith ourselves but received it from outside. Faith always presupposes a crossing of boundaries—going to the others and coming from the others, which, in turn, points to its originating from *the* Other, Jesus Christ.

[107] Irenaeus of Lyons, *Adversus haereses* I, 10, 2.

With respect to the relationship between the universal Church and the particular Church, the bishop has a central role. From the unity of the Sacrament and the Word, he embodies the unity of the local Church (= diocese). At the same time, the bishop is a link to the other local churches: he is responsible for the unity of the Church in his diocese and at the same time has the task of constantly reinvigorating the unity of his local church with the universal Church, the one Church of Jesus Christ.

The bishop bears responsibility—as Joseph Ratzinger said—both for the catholic and for the apostolic dimension of his local church. Although these two essential elements of the Church do especially characterize the episcopal office, they are also directly connected to the other two marks of the Church: being apostolic and being catholic serve her unity, her oneness. Without unity, there is no holiness either. For holiness is essentially realized in the integration of the individual members into the reconciling love of the one Body of Jesus Christ. The purification of a person's own existence through being melded into the all-embracing love of Christ brings about that person's holiness, which is the holiness of the triune God Himself.

The mission of the bishop can be basically paraphrased in terms of what Sacred Scripture calls the will of Jesus regarding the apostles: He appointed them "to be with him, and to be sent out to proclaim the message, and to have authority" (Mark 3:14–15).

The basic prerequisite of episcopal ministry is inner communion with Jesus Christ, a being with Him (*Mit-sein*). The bishop must be a witness to the Resurrection. He must be in touch with the risen Christ. Without this inner being with Christ, he becomes a mere Church official. He would then no longer be a witness and successor to the apostles. Being with Jesus Christ, which presupposes the internalization of faith, also brings about a participation in Jesus' mission. For Christ, with His whole existence, is the messenger who has made His being-with-the-Father into a being-with-people. The mission of the bishop consists, above all, in carrying this being-with-God to the people and in gathering them into this being-with.

Here it becomes clear what the commission to the apostles means when they are given the authority to drive out evil spirits: the arrival of Jesus' mission heals and cleanses people from within. It purifies the atmosphere of the spirit in which they live through the entering in of the Holy Spirit. To be with God through Christ and to bring God to the people: that is the mission of the bishop. Jesus says, "Whoever does not gather with me scatters" (Matt. 12:30). The bishop's task is to gather with Jesus.

A second element follows from this: every bishop is in the apostolic succession. Only the bishop of Rome is the successor of a particular apostle, St. Peter, and he is entrusted with the responsibility for the whole Church. All the other bishops are successors of the Bishops, but not of specific ones. They belong to the college of bishops. The "collegial" aspect is the necessary consequence of the catholic and apostolic dimension of the episcopate.

First of all, there is the special bond between the bishops of a region (the episcopal or bishops' conference) who seek a common path for their episcopal ministry within a shared political and cultural context. This demands both the personal responsibility of each individual bishop and the search for a common witness.

When speaking of the community of the bishops, we must take a further level into account: the college of bishops exists not only synchronously, i.e., in the present, but also diachronically, i.e., across the ages. In this respect, no generation is isolated in the Church.

The bishop does not proclaim ideas of his own devising. Rather, he is a messenger of Jesus Christ. For the bishop, the signpost guiding us into the message is the community of the Church of all times. If a majority were to form somewhere that went against the Faith of the Church as proclaimed throughout the centuries, then this would not constitute a majority in terms of the Faith. The true majority in the Church is diachronic; i.e., it transcends the times. Only those who listen to this whole majority remain in the community of the apostles.

Faith goes beyond the self-absolutization of the respective present. It opens the present to the Faith of all times, thus freeing it from ideological delusions while holding open the future. One important task of the bishop that arises from the communal nature of his office is to be the spokesman for this majority of the faithful across the ages, i.e., to be the voice of the Church uniting the centuries.

The bishop represents the universal Church to his local church and the local church to the universal Church. Thus, he is a servant of unity. He must not allow the local church to shut itself off from the universal Church. Rather, he must open it up to the whole so that the invigorating forces of the respective charisms can flow back and forth. The bishop who opens up and interprets the local church to the universal Church brings to the universal Church the particular voice of his diocese, its particular gifts of grace, its merits and sufferings. Everything belongs to all. The contribution of every local church is important for the good of the universal Church.

The pope, as the successor of St. Peter, must not stifle the special gifts of the individual local churches in the exercise of his office and must not force them into a false uniformity. Rather, he must allow the different charisms of the local churches to take effect in a lively exchange within the whole. The pope should impose only those elements of human law that go beyond the sacred law stemming from the sacrament that are really necessary. The bishop and the bishops' conferences should proceed likewise in their own sphere. They must beware of becoming pastorally uniform. They, too, must bear in mind the rule of St Paul: "Do not quench the Spirit.... But test everything; hold fast to what is good" (1 Thess. 5:19, 21). There must be no uniformization of pastoral planning in the Church. Rather, space must be left—with the proviso of maintaining the unity of faith—for the diversity of God's gifts.

The apostles are always sent "to the ends of the earth." Hence, the bishop's mission can never be restricted to one within the Church. The gospel is intended for all people. It is therefore the responsibility of the successors of the apostles to take it out into the world. The faith must always be proclaimed anew to those who do not yet recognize Christ as their Savior. In addition, the bishops have a responsibility for the affairs of public life.

It is undisputed that the state enjoys an autonomy with respect to the Church. The bishop must recognize the state's own laws. He must avoid mixing faith and politics, and he serves the freedom of all by not allowing the Faith to be identified with any particular form of politics. The gospel sets out truths and values for politics, but it does not answer concrete individual questions in matters of politics and economics. The "independence of temporal affairs"[108] spoken of by Vatican II must be respected by all the faithful. Only in this way can the Church remain an open space for reconciliation to take place between the parties. And only in this way does she avoid becoming a party herself. In this context, respect for the maturity of the laity is also an important aspect of the episcopal ministry.

But the independence enjoyed by temporal affairs is not absolute. Augustine, subsequent to the experiences of the Roman Empire, pointed out that the boundaries between the state and a

---

[108] Second Vatican Council, *Gaudium et spes* 36.

band of robbers become blurred when the state fails to adhere to certain minimum ethical norms. The state does not just produce law. What is wrong in itself, such as the killing of innocent persons, cannot be declared to be a right by any law of the state.

Christians have the urgent task of maintaining the ability within the sphere of political life to hear the voice of creation. The bishop must ensure that people do not grow deaf to the fundamental truths of conscience that God has inscribed in every human heart. St. Gregory the Great said that the bishop must have a good nose, i.e., the sense that enables him to distinguish between right and wrong. This applies to the inner-Church sphere as well as to the sphere of social and political life. It is precisely respect for what belongs to public life as its own that requires the Church to act as an advocate for creation where its voice is being drowned out in the hubbub of self-made things. One of the bishop's outstanding tasks is to awaken people's consciences and make them sensitive to the demands of the times.

Chapter 13

We wait for adoption (as sons), the redemption of our bodies:
adoptionem filiorum Dei exspectantes, redemptionem corporis nostri
Romans 8:23, RSVCE and LV

The hope of bodily resurrection is a cross-check on our understanding of the incarnational and sacramental reality of God's presence in all our being as persons in a spiritual-bodily nature.

"It is sown a physical body, it is raised a spiritual body" (1 Cor. 15:44). Through Christ's Cross and Resurrection, human beings are freed from Adam's sin and its consequence, eternal death. The effect of Christ's suffering is mediated through the sacraments. In Baptism and Reconciliation (and the Anointing of the Sick), the *guilt of sin* and the eternal penalties of sin (but not all the temporal ones) are forgiven. Man enters into a supernatural relationship with God and receives a pledge of future glory through the grace of the sacraments. Only at the end of the world will people receive the full effect of the Resurrection — namely, the overcoming of death as the penalty of sin, when Christ by His power raises all the dead.

Even if reason cannot compel the idea of resurrection, if the argumentation starts from man's being and the meaning of his existence, it can nevertheless make the idea at least plausible. According to the Creator's intention, the soul is created immortal. It is the principle of man's creaturely existence. It realizes the unity of body and spirit and signifies the disposition of man's spiritual and free nature for the reception of supernatural grace. The soul is the continuous bearer of man's created nature in all its moral dispositions and historical modalities. It contradicts the essence of the soul to be outside the matter in which it subsists. If this matter is destroyed in death through the decaying of the body, the soul remains imperfect and, by its nature, calls for the full restoration of corporeal-spiritual integrity. But because such a resurrection is beyond the soul's own powers, only God Himself is able to bring about the resurrection of the human being—i.e., both the restoration of the person's integral nature and its perfection through grace.

On the other side of death, however, man is not produced anew out of nothing by means of God's memory of him, which would mean that there was no natural identity between man in his earthly existence and in his perfection in Heaven. In death, it is only the connection between the constituent principles of individual soul and matter that is severed. The soul, however, remains the principle of identity and the substantial form of the unity of body and soul. Matter remains the ground of possibility into which the soul brings the individuality and personality of a human being and of his or her subsistence. So the soul never exists completely incorporeally because, as the substantial form, it also guarantees the metaphysical identity of the self-expression in matter and thus also the person's bodily identity. In this sense, man rises in his "own body" to eternal life and appears in his material identity with his earthly existence: *in numero idem*. It should be noted here that soul and matter work as metaphysical principles. There is no empirical and quantifiable continuity that could be ascertained by man in the pilgrim state. But if a limb was missing at death, or if the person was physically deformed from the beginning of his or her life, all such deficiencies are removed through God's omnipotence and goodness because, in redeemed and perfected matter, the consequences of sin are so completely overcome that the soul imprints its necessarily three-dimensional formative power on matter. Thus, it is possible for a person's specific physical appearance to correspond to his or her generic physical appearance.

What is the nature of the resurrected body?

This question does not open up a wide field for speculations and phantasmagorias. The aim of the Church's statements of faith is only to hold fast to the reality of the resurrection of the whole human being in body and soul and to accept nothing else as a measure other than being conformed to the transfigured body of Christ. The spiritual tradition of the Church has always adhered to the consoling image that portrays the human body at the age of thirty-three as the ideal of the glorified body of the redeemed. What it has in mind here even more than the biological culmination point is the immediate vision of the transfigured human nature of the God-Man, Jesus Christ. The "measure of the full stature of Christ" (Eph. 4:13) is calculated in its historical expression from the givens that "Jesus, when he began his ministry, was about thirty years of age" (Luke 3:23) and that He spent three years proclaiming the Kingdom of God before His Cross and glorious Resurrection. Here the Father revealed the glory of the Son, and the Son revealed to all the name of the Father, who has given Him "power to give eternal life" to those who believe in Him (see John 17:2).

But what are we to understand by the "spiritual body" of which Paul speaks (1 Cor. 15:42–44) compared with an ethereal body or a soul floating on clouds of ideas in the spirit realm? What Paul "called 'spiritual' is not so because the body itself will be a spirit, but because, with the Spirit giving life, it will remain immortal and incorruptible."[109]

The Resurrection of Christ lays the foundation for the resurrection of all human beings at the end of the world, as well as for their natural and supernatural perfection.[110] The imperishability of those who are resurrected is rooted in their participation in God's eternity. It is not man as a species—which exists only as an idea (or as an uncountable noun or a collective singular)—that participates in God's eternity, but each individual human being, who is a concrete person. This is emphasized to counter the idea of a quasi-immortality with an infinite (biological) procreation series in which the human being is preserved as a species-being while the individual falls prey to death.[111]

In the status of eternal perfection, the male and female sexes will remain because sexuality belongs to the integrity of the nature of the male and female body.[112] For the existence of two sexes is also an expression of the wisdom of the Creator, who arranges the order of what He has created in such a way that the eternal beauty of God shines through the dissimilarity and correspondence of the finite.[113] But, of course, eternal life does not consist in the enjoyment of food, which is no longer necessary for the preservation of the individual life. Furthermore, the end of history means that

[109] Fulgentius of Ruspe, De fide ad Petrum, chap. 29, rule 26, in Selected Works (The Fathers of the Church, vol. 95), 101.
[110] Cf. Thomas Aquinas, Summa contra gentiles IV, 79-97.
[111] So Ludwig Feuerbach, Gedanken über Tod und Unsterblichkeit [1830], in Werke 1, ed. E. Thies (Frankfurt: Suhrkamp, 1975), 76-349;Ludwig Feuerbach, Das Wesen des Christentums [1841], in Werke V, ed. E. Thies (Frankfurt a. M.: Suhrkamp, 1976), 160-165 (Das Geheimnis der Auferstehung und der übernatürlichen Geburt).
[112] Augustine, De civitate Dei 22, 18.
[113] Fulgentius of Ruspe, De fide a Petrum 3, 35.

there is no longer any need for the procreation of offspring, for the sake of which the sexual attraction between the sexes exists. "For in the resurrection they neither marry nor are given in marriage, but are like angels in heaven" (Matt. 22:30).

God Himself will be the source and pinnacle of all the joy that fills the soul and also meets with a response in physical existence. Man's natural desire for the vision of God finds its fulfillment in love. Man does, in fact, see God directly, but in a creaturely way, mediated through the humanity of Jesus.

Man arises from death in his true body, not in an ethereal construct. He is endowed with bridal gifts through which the soul can more suitably consummate its nuptial union with the life of God. The bridal gifts of the soul are the vision, the love, and the enjoyment of God. The bodily gifts are freedom from suffering and the best possible adaptation of the body to the soul.

What is our final destiny?

We know that all things work together for good for those who love God, who are called according to his purpose. For those whom he foreknew he also predestined to be conformed to the image of his Son, in order that he might be the firstborn within a large family. And those whom he predestined he also called; and those whom he called he also justified; and those whom he justified he also glorified.

What then are we to say about these things? If God is for us, who is against us? He who did not withhold his own Son, but gave him up for all of us, will he not with him also give us everything else? Who will bring any charge against God's elect? It is God who justifies. Who is to condemn? It is Christ Jesus, who died, yes, who was raised, who is at the right hand of God, who indeed intercedes for us. Who will separate us from the love of Christ? Will hardship, or distress, or persecution, or famine, or nakedness, or peril, or sword? As it is written,

> "For your sake we are being killed all day long;
> we are accounted as sheep to be slaughtered."

No, in all these things we are more than conquerors through him who loved us. For I am convinced that neither death, nor life, nor angels, nor rulers, nor things present, nor things to come, nor powers, nor height, nor depth, nor anything else in all creation, will be able to separate us from the love of God in Christ Jesus our Lord. (Rom. 8:28-39)

Chapter 14

Behold God's tent among the people

Revelation 21:3

In my Father's house there are many dwelling-places. If it were not so, would I have told you that I go to prepare a place for you? And if I go and prepare a place for you, I will come again and will take you to myself, so that where I am, there you may be also. (John 14:2–3)

"Heaven" is where the self-communication of God is accepted or the longing for God is graciously fulfilled in the mode of inalienability.

At the Last Judgment, Christ says to the redeemed from the throne of His glory: "Come, you that are blessed by my Father, inherit the kingdom prepared for you from the foundation of the world" (Matt. 25:34; cf. Rev. 20:11–15).

The goal toward which man is journeying by nature—i.e., on account of his creatureliness—cannot be found in a subsequent state of the carefree enjoyment of spiritual and sensual pleasures distinct from God. Man's goal is God Himself; and Heaven is the Kingdom of God, which has fully come to us. In Heaven, man meets God Himself as the content of his bliss, of his eternal happiness and unceasing joy. And in God, he at the same time finds himself in the community of all the saved. He does not experience the communion realized with all the saints as an external add-on, as a secondary source of blessedness, as it were. God is the one source of love that suffuses everything and everyone, flooding through the social connections between the saints as the Nile floods its delta. Thus, love of neighbor is not a supplement to love of God but rather the latter's taking shape in the direction of someone else who has been redeemed. Communion among the blessed does not contradict the comprehensively theocentric and Christocentric nature of creation in its redeemed form. Every saint is recognized only in God, and every love of Him knows itself to emanate from and be carried by God's Spirit while being directed toward God. Then God does not see the beloved human being as a competitor. We have no need to fear that God might become jealous of us if we love our neighbor too much. God Himself honors those who serve Him: "Whoever serves me, the Father will honour" (John 12:26). God has no need of being honored by His creatures. He glorifies Himself in His acts of creation and redemption, in that the Father glorifies the Son and the Son glorifies the Father in the revelation of God's triune love.

For the glory of God is a living man; and the life of man consists in beholding God.[114]

This thought also underlies the Christian veneration of the saints. They are not further focuses or addressees of piety alongside God and Christ. In them, the believer here on earth honors the power of God's transforming grace. Any honor accorded to them, especially the recognition of their example, honors God in them.[115] The intercession for which we are permitted to ask them is also premised on the assumption that all God's grace and His help in everyday life stem from Him alone but that He links some of His

---

[114] Irenaeus of Lyon, *Adversus haereses* IV, 20, 7.
[115] See DH 675.

gifts to the intercessory prayer of the saints in order to make the social and human dimension of salvation clear.

Heaven means participating in the life of the triune God. In and with the Incarnate Son, we recognize God as He is, in the contemplation of His essentiality, which subsists in the three Divine Persons. We allow our will to be moved to participate in the community of the love of the Father and the Son in the Holy Spirit that has been given to us (Rom. 5:5).

But do we exhaust the mystery of the triune God through our full knowledge of God, which transforms faith into vision and hope into the experience of the presence of salvation, and through our complete and liberated love of God?

Here we have to bear in mind the extent and limits of our finite knowledge, which remains, by its very nature, finite and creaturely even when it has been elevated above itself in the Logos and the Holy Spirit to an activity that it would not be capable of by itself. God has shown Himself in His revelation. After our death, He is no longer accepted and believed merely through creaturely conceptual images but shows Himself to us in His essentiality, through which we know Him and therefore become aware of Him in the mode of seeing, i.e., directly. The limitation of our finite knowledge, on the other hand, lies in the fact that we do not know God in a divine way but in our creaturely way. Thus, we do indeed grasp God as the object of our vision, but precisely as the inconceivable depth of His Trinitarian reality as Person (*Person-Wirklichkeit*).

So although our vision of God has always already reached its goal, it has nevertheless done so in such a way that its present is at the same time also its future as a dynamic and blissful, unfathomable, mysterious *Woraufhin* — "toward which." But then, if our creaturely reality is and remains incarnationally shaped by God's Incarnation, we must also confess that the human nature of the

God's Presence in the Eucharist and in the World

Logos, into which we are constituted through the grace of participation, remains eternally as man's *Worin*—wherein (medium)—and *Woraufhin* (tendency) toward the triune God. In God "we live and move and have our being" (Acts 17:28).

Eternal life is not the tormenting over and over again of a never-ending time as the measure of material movement but, rather, perfect and fulfilling community with God. That is why the definitive form of our being is called *life*, since it is not only a matter of a purely de facto existence in the way that a stone exists or an oak tree becomes "ancient." *Life* means that deep determination of a being that enables it to have an interiority toward itself, to possess itself (*Selbsthabe* = having self) and to behave freely toward something else. In the highest sense, life belongs to the person. Through the two fundamental activities of the intellect, those of reason and of the will, the human person reaches his or her goal in community with God. Sharing in performing God's absolute activeness, insofar as God is pure acting reality, means a fulfilled life in the most extensive and intensive sense conceivable.

Just as there is an absolute difference between God and what is created in their being-hood (*Seinshabe* = having being), so eternity and time must be understood to be given as the fitting modes of being of God and the creature. God's absolute identity with Himself—i.e., His being and self-enactment—is called God's eternity. Since we do not know God in His essence, through which He is God, we do not know in the very truest sense what eternity is. We only have an analogous knowledge through its outward effects through being (*Sein*), in which all who exist (*alle Seienden*) have their existence through participation and are determined in their essence (*Wesen*) by the degree of their participation in being (*Seins-Teilhabe*).

The fact that every finite existence must first recapture its fullness through realizing its possibilities—with which it is not identical—is the reason finite being is experienced in a mode of actualization that we call *time*. Man's actualization in the succession of moments is his temporality and finitude. When we conclude our history of freedom in death, we are not able to leave behind the mode of being of time as such. It merely loses that which is dispersing, disintegrating, which is unbordered, fraying, and melting. The difference between existence and essence, between being and the activity of our faculties of intellect and freedom remains; otherwise, we would have to become identical with God. Only in God do being and life become completely one. God's self-communication in Christ, in which He revealed Himself in His resolve for us, establishes the inalienability of our act of being (*Seins-Akt*), which makes us the individual human beings that we are. Nevertheless, we are essentially different from God and not essentially eternal but only eternal *per analogiam et participationem*. This, however, also makes it possible for us to realize the capacities of our intellect and will, which have an effect that goes beyond themselves to a personal-dialogical participation in the enactment of God's life, in His self-knowledge in the eternal Word and His love for Himself in the Holy Spirit, whose divine name in which He reveals Himself is faith (1 Cor. 13:13) or love (Rom. 5:5). In this, the person who is saved lives eternally in his or her sharing in the enactment of the Trinitarian processions and relations of God-eternity.

Our Christian faith is total surrender to the triune God in the love that the Father of Jesus Christ has poured into our hearts through the Holy Spirit (Rom. 5:5). When we look at Christ on the Cross, we are filled with a direct certainty that every human life is significant. Everyone here in our circle—you and I, all of us together and each of us individually—should feel themselves addressed directly as a person created in God's image and likeness in their life and thinking, hoping and suffering, in their relationships with their loved ones and their enemies, when Jesus says: "For God so loved the world that he gave his only Son, so that everyone who believes in him may not perish but may have eternal life" (John 3:16).

This is neither the love of romantic feelings nor the calculated compassion that obeys the rule of *do ut des*, out through whose seams nihilism peeps or the venom of cynicism seeps. God's love is redeeming and re-creating because God gains nothing and loses nothing when He communicates Himself to us in the Cross and Resurrection of His Son. He gives Himself to us as the truth through which we know Him and the life in which we become one with Him. Those whose thinking follows the norms of the world and who therefore declare money and fame, power and luxury to be their elixir of life are bound to turn away in disappointment and horror from a God hanging on the Cross. And those who define God religiously and philosophically as absolute superiority and self-sufficient thinking will shudder at the "word of the cross" (1 Cor. 1:18, RSVCE) as expressing an immature or primitive idea of God. "But we proclaim Christ crucified, a stumbling-block to Jews and foolishness to Gentiles, but to those who are the called, both Jews and Greeks, Christ the power of God and the wisdom of God. For God's foolishness is wiser than human wisdom, and God's weakness is stronger than human strength" (1 Cor. 1:23-25).

Given the power of political and ideological atheism and the religiously based enmity toward the Church of Christ all over the world, the cause of Christ seems lost—as it once did on Golgotha, when Jesus was mocked with the cynical words: "If you are the Son of God, come down from the cross ..., and we will believe in

[you]" (Matt. 27:40, 42). According to human criteria, the Church is fighting a losing battle.

But all those who once wielded their power over life and death historically against Jesus and persecuted His disciples over the ages are today forgotten or are remembered for their evil deeds and have had to stand trial before the just and yet also forgiving God. Jesus, however, lives. He alone can overcome our death, too, and open the hearts of the persecutors to His love.

Let us therefore stand faithfully by the Cross of Jesus, even if we are ridiculed as being medieval by those who have power over how people think and live or even if we are opposed and demotivated inside the Church by secularized fellow Christians who call us out of date and out of touch with reality. We bend our knees before the name of Jesus alone. We confess Him who was obedient to the point of death on the Cross. For "Jesus Christ is Lord, to the glory of God the Father" (Phil. 2:8, 11).

> And I saw the holy city, the new Jerusalem, coming down out of heaven from God, prepared as a bride adorned for her husband. And I heard a loud voice from the throne saying,
>
> > "See, the home of God is among mortals.
> > He will dwell with them;
> > they will be his peoples,
> > and God himself will be with them;
> > he will wipe every tear from their eyes.
> > Death will be no more;
> > mourning and crying and pain will be no more,
> > for the first things have passed away."
>
> And the one who was seated on the throne said, "See, I am making all things new." (Rev. 21:2-5)

Homily at the conclusion
of the spiritual retreat

During the days of this spiritual retreat, we have opened our hearts and minds to the mystery of God's real presence: in the creation of the world, in the history of His Chosen People, in His Word made flesh, in the Holy Church, in the Eucharist, and in the promise of eternal life. In the Most Holy Sacrament of the Altar, Christ, through the Holy Spirit, takes us into His sacrifice to the Father for the salvation of the world. The eternal Son of the Father is, in His human nature, the real presence of the triune God in the midst of us human beings. He said: "Whoever has seen me has seen the Father" (John 14:9). In his human nature, He is our way to the Father, and in His divine nature, He is the goal as our life in the truth (John 14:6). In His Divine Person, He is the revealed truth. He gives us life as children of God. His disciples follow Him when they walk the path of earthly life and—thanks to the gift of perseverance—do not leave Him right up to the day when they arrive at the house of the eternal Father (see John 14:2). By freely accepting our different charisms as members of His Body, we build up the Body of Christ "until all of us come to the unity of the faith and of the knowledge of the Son of God, to maturity, to the measure of the full stature of Christ" (Eph. 4:13).

God's Presence in the Eucharist and in the World

Dear confreres, today you are reaffirming your willingness to offer your whole being and life as a sacrifice to God. This is therefore also a time of grace for the entire People of God. In the sacramental priesthood, we are linked to all the faithful by virtue of the common priesthood: "Each of them in its own special way is a participation in the one priesthood of Christ."[116]

The one, holy, catholic, and apostolic Church, to which we belong through Baptism and Confirmation and which we serve as shepherds in the name of Christ, is instituted by God. Therefore the "gates of Hades will not prevail against it" (Matt. 16:18).

But the Church is made up of us weak and sinful human beings. She finds herself—looking at her human side—in a constant crisis of credibility. At this dramatic moment in time, we are expecting and fearing the possible negative consequences of scandals. Jesus said to His disciples, "Occasions for stumbling are bound to come," adding the warning, "but woe to anyone by whom they come" (Luke 17:1). With this, He wanted to remind us of our individual responsibility.

It is not "clericalism," whatever that may be, but rather the turning away from truth and the condoning of moral licentiousness that are the roots of evil. The corruption of doctrine always entails and manifests itself in the corruption of morals. Grave sin committed without any qualms of conscience against the sanctity of the Church results from the relativization of the dogmatic foundation of the Church. This is the real cause that lies behind the shock and dismay felt by millions of faithful Catholics. In his analysis of the causes of the secessions from the one Church of Christ in the sixteenth century, the Church historian Hubert Jedin (1900–1980) stated in the first volume of his *History of the*

---

[116] Second Vatican Council, *Lumen gentium* 10.

Council of Trent: "The word 'reform' masked the heresy and the nascent schism."[117]

Then as now, there was much talk of reform. However, then as now, true reform of the Church in the spirit of Christ is not secularization of the Church but rather the sanctification of human beings by God so as to serve the coming of His Kingdom.

Salvation from sin is grounded in the truth that Jesus is the Son of God. Without the historical fact of the Incarnation, the Church would dwindle into nothing more than an intraworldly agency for the improvement of the world. She would no longer have any significance for our yearning for God and our longing for eternal life. The priest would be merely a functionary in a socioreligious movement of a romantic or revolutionary nature. The Church does not increase her relevance and acceptance by serving the world as a trainbearer for the spirit of the age but only by walking ahead of it, bearing the torch of the truth of Christ. We should not try to impress with secondary issues and work on the agendas of others who refuse to believe that God alone is the origin and the sole goal of mankind and of all creation.

For there is also a real danger facing humanity today that lies in the greenhouse gases of sin and the global warming of unbelief, as well as in the post-humanist negation of man's being made in the image and likeness of God and finally in the breakdown of morality when no one knows or teaches the difference between

---

[117] Hubert Jedin, *Geschichte des Konzils von Trient I* (Freiburg i. Br.: Herder, 1977), 151; English: *A History of the Council of Trent*, vol. 1 (Edinburgh: Thomas Nelson, 1957), 187; cf. Gerhard Kardinal Müller, *Der Papst. Sendung und Auftrag* (Freiburg i. Br.: Herder, 2017), 131–135.

good and evil any longer. The best environmentalist and lover of nature is the person who proclaims the gospel and its eternal truth that God alone brings about the survival of man and nature, doing so not just for a limited time and the near future but forever and ever.

In the opinion that Christian dogma no longer constitutes the ground and criterion for morality and pastoral care, there emerges a Christological heresy—namely, that of setting Christ the Teacher of the divine truth in opposition to Christ the Good Shepherd. A good doctor can help us only combined with the effective medicine. For it is one and the same Christ who says of Himself: "I am the way, and the truth, and the life" (John 14:6) and who also reveals Himself to be in His Person the *Pastor Bonus*, the pastoral carer of the Church, when He unveils the mystery of His Person and mission: "I am the good shepherd. The good shepherd lays down his life for the sheep" (John 10:11).

A true pray-er and pastor is one who looks with the love of God upon the people entrusted to him and takes his bearings in his spiritual ministry and Christ-shaped way of life from the High Priest of the New and Everlasting Covenant. The good shepherd is radically different from the hireling because he loves his people with the heart of Jesus and lays down his life for the Lord's flock. Apostles are "servants of Christ and stewards of God's mysteries" (1 Cor. 4:1) and "work together with him" (2 Cor. 6:1). They have one concern: "knowing the fear of the Lord, we try to persuade others" (2 Cor. 5:11).

Spiritual retreats are crowned with success when we joyfully and freely allow ourselves to be inspired by the Apostle to be conformed to Christ: "Clothe yourselves with the new self, created according to the likeness of God in true righteousness and holiness.... Therefore be imitators of God, as beloved children, and live in love, as Christ loved us and gave himself up for us, a fragrant offering and sacrifice to God" (Eph. 4:24; 5:1–2). Amen.[118]

---

[118] Original version in the sermon given in Tarnów.

Epilogue

We began our spiritual retreat with a prayer of St. Ignatius of Loyola. And we conclude our reflections on the Real Presence of God in His creation, in the Church, and in the Eucharist with a mystical prayer on the healing power of patience written by the Doctor of the Church Teresa of Ávila:[119]

Nada te turbe	Let nothing disturb you,
Nada te espante,	Let nothing frighten you,
Todo se pasa,	All things pass away:
Dios no se muda,	God never changes.
La paciencia	Patience obtains all
Todo lo alcanza;	things.
Quien a Dios tiene	He who has God
Nada le falta:	Finds he lacks nothing;
Sólo Dios basta.	God alone suffices.

[119] Santa Teresa de Jesús, *Obras Completas* (Madrid: Editorial Católica, 1986), 667.

About the Author

Gerhard Ludwig Müller (b. 1947) is the archbishop emeritus of Regensburg, Germany. The second German after Joseph Ratzinger to lead the Congregation for the Doctrine of the Faith, he has a profound knowledge of modern theology and has dedicated his life to the study of Christian comprehension of revelation, ecclesiology, and ecumenism.

THE
NEUMANN✠FORUM

The Mission
The Neumann Forum unites and engages faithful
Catholics who are dedicated to preserving and
protecting the Catholic Faith.

Sophia Institute

Sophia Institute is a nonprofit institution that seeks to nurture the spiritual, moral, and cultural life of souls and to spread the gospel of Christ in conformity with the authentic teachings of the Roman Catholic Church.

Sophia Institute Press fulfills this mission by offering translations, reprints, and new publications that afford readers a rich source of the enduring wisdom of mankind.

Sophia Institute also operates the popular online resource CatholicExchange.com. *Catholic Exchange* provides world news from a Catholic perspective as well as daily devotionals and articles that will help readers to grow in holiness and live a life consistent with the teachings of the Church.

In 2013, Sophia Institute launched Sophia Teachers to renew and rebuild Catholic culture through service to Catholic education. With the goal of nurturing the spiritual, moral, and cultural life of souls, and an abiding respect for the role and work of teachers, we strive to provide materials and programs that are at once enlightening to the mind and ennobling to the heart; faithful and complete, as well as useful and practical.

Sophia Institute gratefully recognizes the Solidarity Association for preserving and encouraging the growth of our apostolate over the course of many years. Without their generous and timely support, this book would not be in your hands.

www.SophiaInstitute.com
www.CatholicExchange.com
www.SophiaTeachers.org

Sophia Institute Press is a registered trademark of Sophia Institute.
Sophia Institute is a tax-exempt institution as defined by the
Internal Revenue Code, Section 501(c)(3). Tax ID 22-2548708.